...Who You *Truly* Are

Endorsements

"*Don't Forget to Remember* is a heartbreaking, yet inspirational account of one woman's journey navigating through love, loss, and devastation. Colleen writes a beautiful story about her personal breakthroughs as she overcomes disloyalty and betrayal from the people closest to her heart. It's her story to share as she truly learns to love herself, wearing her battle scars like wings. I highly recommend this, it is truly a wonderful read."

Judy O'Beirn
CEO & President of
Hasmark Publishing International

"Loved this book, it was a joy to read. I felt as if Colleen and I were just sitting together on a couch talking and sharing life, the ups and downs. She keeps asking herself the same questions I ask myself. Wow. I highly recommend this book."

Ann Collins
International bestselling author
Hope Loss enCourage

DON'T FORGET TO REMEMBER...

...Who You *Truly* Are

Colleen K. Buchanan

Hasmark Publishing
www.hasmarkpublishing.com
Copyright © 2021 Colleen K. Buchanan

First Edition

Disclaimer

Permission should be addressed in writing to Colleen at buchananlee578@gmail.com

Editor: Judith Scott
judith@hasmarkpublishing.com
Cover Layout: Anne Karklins
anne@hasmarkpublishing.com
Interior layout: AmitDey
amit@hasmarkpublishing.com

ISBN 13: 978-1-989756-98-0
ISBN 10: 1989756980

Dedication

I am dedicating this book to ME.

Acknowledgements

I would like to thank Patti, Cheick, Jen, Isobel, Kim, Pam and Max for always being there to listen and support me through all the pain and laugher. I love you all. A very special and heartfelt thank you to everyone at Hasmark Publishing: Judy O'Beirn, Jenna Ventura, Judith Scott, and Anne Karklins for bringing this book to publication. I especially want to thank my lawyer for her generosity of time, belief in this book, and encouragement.

Table of Contents

CHAPTER 1

Learning About Myself and How to Accept and Let Go of the Past

September 2018

Sunday

My mind just cracked, big time, and for the second time in two years! I wasn't just suffering from mental overload, but physical overload too. I really wish I could explain the panic within myself that I have been living through. Even as I type this, my jaw is tight, I'm fighting through a panic attack, and my entire body is rigid and tense. I've been doing things I don't want to do, seeing people I don't want to see, ignoring my cats, not going to yoga (the one thing that brings me bliss), and wasting hours playing solitaire.

I had a dream once. Unfortunately, I got way too bloody challenged by what the Universe was giving me in order for that dream to materialize. Can I really do this? Can I write my story for the third time? They do say the third time's a charm. So, here's to being charmed. For over forty years, I lived a life full of lies and secrets. My first attempt at writing my story took me two years to complete. But it wasn't my truth. I was still living a lie and holding onto the past and my demons. I finally found the courage to speak up, but it came with a price. My second attempt writing about my life was a phenomenal success. When I submitted it to a publisher, they told me they were interested in publishing it – talk about a dream come true! And again, it took me two years to write. And yet, after submitting it, I didn't feel like I'd prevailed or even found the closure I needed.

Too many of us are involved with people in our lives who aren't supportive and force us to be someone we are not. I probably shouldn't say "force us" because we do have a choice. But that choice sometimes means losing people we've known all our lives. This is what's so hard about living your truth – not caring what anyone else will think about you or how they will judge you – regardless of whether they are family members or close friends. The only time it matters is if you've chosen to bring a life into this world. You are their example. What example are you teaching your children?

So, how does one write one's truth when what happens in the house should stay in the house? By, hopefully, coming from a place of integrity. This is my journey about how I learned to love myself and know that I've always been worthy of love and that I am pure love. I haven't given up on my dreams, nor will I ever. I just have more work to do on myself than I'd imagined after having finished the second book. I learned that I do not like myself – so let's not even talk about loving myself – and that was terrifying to understand.

To save me time, I'll just include parts of the second manuscript (book two) that addressed why I have lived most of my life in fear, confusion, and loathing.

Excerpt from Book Two:

December 2016

Friday

Eight days ago, I was at a point of questioning my life's relevance – something, I believe, many of us have experienced. I saw a doctor who changed the medication I was on (I've been on anxiety meds for years. I experienced my first panic attack in my late twenties) and recommended specific therapy for me. What made me question my life's worth? The secrets I'd kept for over four decades. Let's back up a bit.

Almost four years ago, I got myself fired from my job. I'd worked there for almost two and a half years and should have quit after the first six months, but it had taken me a while to find this job, and it fit with what I was looking for at the time (except for being happy at work). I was devastated to be fired! Never, in my life, had that happened to me. It didn't matter that I hated the place; it was a paycheque that I relied on. It didn't matter that it was my own fault; it was demoralizing. I spent months looking for another job, but my heart wasn't in it at all. Being fired had hurt me personally, and I started questioning myself and my life and seeing just how unhappy I was. So, with no prospects of any work and feeling horrible about myself, I spoke with someone who suggested I write about everything I was keeping bottled up inside of me.

More than a dozen years ago, my Mum died of cancer. That's when my life stopped, and I changed in a way I've never truly recovered from. My Mum was my world – she meant everything to me. I was living in a different country at the time, and I went home to be her primary caregiver for her last months of life. Everything I saw and experienced during that period traumatized me. When she died, I numbed myself from the pain. I'd lost my father a few years earlier and still hadn't dealt with his death, so with my Mum's passing, I truly couldn't cope. Unfortunately, I still can't cope and find ways to numb my emotions or feelings.

My parents' generation never discussed their feelings and/or emotions because they weren't taught how to express themselves honestly. In their time, you did what you were told, got married, got a good job, had kids, and life was beautiful – or so it seemed from the outside looking in. They were ill-prepared for the reality of their own children behaving differently.

Somebody sexually abused me as a child. And no, it was *not* my Dad (miss you, Dad). We pretended it didn't happen. I knew it happened, so couldn't understand what the pretending was all about. I acted out horribly as a child and teenager. I did some very, very bad things. But I was acting out because of what happened to me. I started stealing and lying shortly after the abuse, and it didn't stop until I was in my late teens, long after the abuse had stopped. I can't even tell you how many times I was told during my childhood and teens what a bad girl I was. There was a very good reason for my destructive behaviours, but my parents never related it to the abuse. I often wondered if my parents believed that because the abuse happened when I was so young, I wouldn't remember it. They were wrong if that was the case. I just kept acting out, and was repeatedly told to "be a good girl." I grew up believing I'd been such a bad child that I'd caused the abuse. To this day, I catch myself telling myself what a "bad girl" I am.

I started skipping school in grade two when I was seven. I was sent to a French school from grades one to three. I refused to speak French and hated being there. I'd hide behind a bush when the bus came and walk back home, and then my Mum would have to drive me to school. I did absolutely no work in that school, and I was called stupid and often hit with a ruler.

Nothing changed when I was transferred to the English elementary school (having to repeat grade three as I was behind) but at least I wasn't called stupid or hit with a ruler. I continued to skip school all the way through college. Where did I go and what did I do when I skipped school? I went home and watched TV. I had a babysitter until grade six, and so once in high school, I would go home to an empty house and watch TV. I would forge my parents' signature to explain my absences. Of course, I got caught and was grounded, but that didn't bother me (as I was always being grounded for something). My Mum kept all my report cards from grades one through college. The following is my high school graduation report:

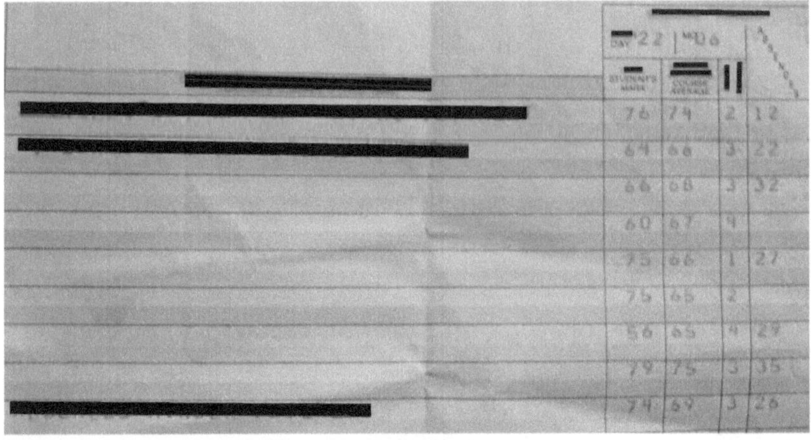

The inconsistent and high number of absences is very interesting, isn't it? I mean, look at the disparity: One subject had only twelve absences and another had thirty-five! Thirty-five? That was my math class. There was a remark that said "absences hinder progress." Really? The only two subjects I never skipped were English, with a mark of 60%, and French, with a mark of 75% (higher than the average by ten points – talk about irony).

And then I turned fifty. You know, the age at which you start re-evaluating your life. I'd kept the denial going for decades, and that constant repression brought me to question the reason for my life.

End of Excerpt

September 2018

Sunday

No wonder I didn't think I'd be able to write a third book if I had to go to that place yet again. So, what brought my mind to breaking again? I am still scared. I quit my job last Friday. It was just way too chaotic for my brain and body to be immersed in. I've been working for over thirty years now, and I know what works for me. I have no problem being busy, but not over-whelmingly busy. But the people were wonderful. And that's what I'd been asking the Universe for – to bring me positive-energy people I could connect with. My coworkers' energies were beautiful. For the first time ever, I was surrounded by so many loving, supportive, caring, and understanding people. In most of my previous jobs, my experiences had been surrounded by too much negative energy, causing me exhaustion. This is an issue that most people don't contemplate: that we are energy.

We all give off energetic vibes. The energy you surround yourself with affects you (and everyone else around you).

One of the owners even told me about an opportunity for a part-time job. Somebody she knew had been looking for someone, but she didn't know if the position had been filled. It's not every day you quit your job and the owner is recommending you for another job.

When I left work for the last time, I had my hair highlighted. New me, new beginning.

The woman before my appointment was late, so the stylist started on me. When the woman finally arrived, she had to wait until I was done. She joined our conversation, and the stylist asked this woman if she knew of a position for me. She gave me the name of a woman who worked in human resources whom she knew, but she didn't know if the company was hiring. Thanks, Universe!

Excerpt from Book Two:

January 2017

Thursday

As if dealing with sexual abuse wasn't enough, I also have no sense of self. I'm black, and I was adopted into a white family when I was just over a year old. You'd think there'd be no denying the colour of my skin. Wrong! I did.

My Mum told me this ostensibly cute story. Apparently, when I was five, I asked my Mum when I was going to turn white. Cute? No, not at all! Very sad and telling, actually. My Mum's response was to take me to an all-black church. And that was supposed to help me how exactly? There were no black families where I lived. All my friends were white. White was all I saw and knew. And I wished I were white!

From a very early age, I never felt normal because I knew I was different. I had lots of friends growing up, and no one ever made me feel as if I didn't belong, but there was always this longing to look like everyone else. My Mum just didn't understand the turmoil I was going through because I never told her about it. The abuse was never talked about, so what was I going to say about my colour? "Mum, I don't want to be black anymore. Mum, why am I always the only black person wherever I go? Mum, I don't understand who I am!" I knew my colour was never going to change, but I was embarrassed about being black.

Things got even harder when I was in high school. Yes, there were black kids in my school, but they were not my friends. I associated only with the white kids. Eventually and naturally, my friends started dating – not me though. When I was a teenager, my Mum took me to a black party. It was nowhere near where we lived, and my Mum told me she'd be staying the entire time (too far to go home and then come back and pick me up). I didn't have a choice. We got there super early, and I helped set up, and when all these black strangers arrived, I told my Mum I'd had enough and made her take me home, missing the entire dance. I didn't consider black people to be *my* people. How could I? I kept all my emotions inside and pretended it didn't matter because I didn't know how to talk about it.

My liberation came when I moved to a different country in my mid-twenties. I needed to leave my home country. I just wanted to be alone. Nobody understood why I needed to do this for myself. I knew no one in the new country and had no support at hand. I know my parents were worried about me, but I desperately needed my own space to learn who I was away from everyone.

When I arrived at my destination, I went through culture shock. I'd never seen and been around so many black professional people. Holy cow! I finally belong! Well, I thought I did until all the friends I made who were black (boyfriends included) called me the black-white girl. Uh huh. I looked black but was told I "acted and talked white," as if it were a bad thing! Ahh, come on! Yup, once again, I didn't fit in.

They made fun of the music I loved: I grew up listening to David Bowie (loved him so much that I named my second kitty after him), Blondie, the Eurythmics, and alternative rock. My new friends took it upon themselves to educate me on what they considered proper music – such as reggae and hip-hop – as if there were something wrong with me for never having listened to these forms of music before, as if the type of music I identified with made me who I was.

I've never had a sense of self because I've never had anyone or anything to identify with. I can't remember when – maybe year five in the new country – I started getting panic attacks. I had no idea what was happening to me. Talk about a brutally scary experience. I really thought I was having a heart attack. I went to a shrink who put me on meds, and they helped tremendously. I tried to open up about the abuse and my fears, but I wasn't ready. I asked the shrink to help me wean myself off the meds and told him I felt fine (denial). Once my Mum died, I needed the meds again.

End of Excerpt

October 2018

Monday

It's my first day no longer working. I thought I'd magically wake up and feel as light as a feather and have no more rigidity or stiffness in my body and that my jaw would no longer be clenched. Apparently, I was wrong. I feel just as terrible as I've been feeling for weeks now. It happens when I have to make life-changing decisions and I'm wracked with doubt, despite what my mind and body are so clearly telling me: This job is not right for you.

If I know what makes me feel happy, peaceful, and calm, why do I not live from this place? Quitting that job was the right thing to do, and yet I still have doubts. Now what do I do? I am trying to believe that the Universe is guiding me to be who I was always meant to be. I am trying to learn that I create my world with my thoughts and actions. I am trying to believe that I can transform my dreams into reality if I let go of who I am not. So how do I do this? There's no quick fix here.

I've always loved self-help books. They inspire me, make me believe I'm doing the right thing, and that all will be well as long as I follow someone else's path, which is why the self-help industry is worth billions. And here I am, about to add to that billion-dollar industry − with a difference, of course. I've spent the past years trying to heal myself. What I've learned is that nobody can teach *you* how to be happy. In order for you to heal completely, you have to release your past traumas from your core, and in my case, that's not something that happens overnight, especially if you've kept everything hidden for over four decades.

Excerpt from Book Two:

January 2017

Thursday

When I was of legal age, I came home from school one day and received a bombshell. My Mum told me that my birth parents wanted to meet me. What the hell? Apparently, they'd put it in the adoption papers that when I was of legal age, they could request a meeting with me. I told my Mum that I had absolutely no interest in meeting them. Just because they were ready to meet me didn't mean I was ready to meet them. But my Mum insisted, and a lunch was set up within weeks.

I met them, and from my perspective it was a disaster! I was polite, as were they, but I just wanted to leave. I had absolutely nothing to say to them. I think it lasted an hour. They'd had almost two decades to prepare, whereas I'd had weeks. When I got home, I think I spoke to my Mum about the encounter for, maybe, ten minutes. Fast-forward to my thirties, and I decided I was ready to re-meet my birth mother. I contacted the adoption agency and was given her coordinates (in the Caribbean). I took a holiday and spent a few days with her. It wasn't what I'd hoped it would be. I really tried to feel something for her, but I didn't. I understood that my identity had nothing to do with her. She couldn't help me understand who I am. I never told my Mum about that second meeting. I felt so much guilt about that. It wasn't until I was in my thirties that I told my Mum about how wrong she'd been to force me to meet my birth parents. I recall that my Mum apologized, telling me she'd thought she was doing the right thing. Right thing for whom? Certainly not me.

End of Excerpt

Nobody knows what the right thing is, but I think my wishes should have been heard, as that experience left me traumatized. I wonder if maybe my Mum was afraid my birth parents would think she was keeping me from them. I'll never know because we never talked about our true feelings.

November 2018

Thursday

My mind was just blown away by someone's absolute forgiveness and caring.

I fell out of friendship with someone whom I had to talk to today. I decided not to be so angry and combative (anger is justified, but useless). We really talked, and I apologized. (Note my friend didn't apologize! Hmph!) This person mentioned a possible employment opportunity to me. Even after all this time, and my nastiness, she was still willing to vouch for my character!

I am so blessed! I am so grateful!

In less than one week, three people have offered to help me find a job! Thanks, Universe.

Friday

My mood has completely switched due to a conversation that had me angry, sad, and disappointed. My trust has been betrayed, again. Learning of the betrayal set me off. I reacted with self-preservation and fear. I feel horribly guilty for having been so awful to someone! Worse, really, than having been betrayed! Just yesterday, someone forgave me and showed me love. And I couldn't pay it forward.

Saturday

I've met a new friend – SAF – and she called me yesterday. I've shared a bit of my life with her, and she's shared a great deal of her story with me, and it's heartbreaking. She was amazed at my ability to pick myself back up and my desire to keep writing.

Monday

It's crucial to understand your beliefs. Are they really yours? I read my horoscope and have seen psychics. Did I just lose you there? Do you believe horoscopes and psychics are fake and a scam? That's ok, those are your beliefs. I don't believe in organized religions or going to church. Nobody's wrong, we just have different views. I do, however, believe in spirituality.

I sometimes wonder what my Mum would make of my spirituality. I grew up in a very religious household. I don't know how or why, but I questioned my religion at an early age. I believed there had to be more to life than what my religion insisted was the truth. I know it hurt my Mum that I was never confirmed in church because we talked about it. I think I took one or two lessons, but I was rebellious, so I quit. I overheard the minister telling my Mum I wasn't ready. No kidding I wasn't ready! I had too many questions and no answers. My parents' religious beliefs weren't mine, which created tension and guilt within me for years. I thought I was bad for having different opinions.

Wednesday

I woke up from a dream around three o'clock this morning. I got a message from the Universe. I started thinking about it and texted myself at 3:05 am so I wouldn't forget. I have no idea what I was dreaming about, but all of a sudden I heard, "Be still and know that I am God." I have no idea how long ago I wrote the following down to understand its meaning, but I know it was when I was living in that other country. It's from Guy Finley's book *The Essential Laws of Fearless Living – Find the Power to Never Feel Powerless Again*:

Be still: Cease from thinking about what you see, and "know" without thinking about it – that no real distance exists between the seer and the seen. The beauty or ugliness that you see near or far is none other than self.

And know: Realize that there is no real distinction between what you perceive about something and what you receive from it in the same moment. Life is a reflection of the consciousness that reveals it. Nothing exists outside of this.

That I AM God: I am not just the life source of all that has been or ever will be seen, but I am the seer as well "that dwells within you". Your true self is seer and seen at once. (Finley, 2008)

Excerpt from Book Two:

February 2017

I had the following dream: I can't tell you how it started (Isn't that always the way with dreams?), but suddenly, I was standing attached to this guy on some platform where we were about to jump in tandem down a very deep waterfall. I was freaking out saying, "I don't know why I'm here! I'm terrified of heights! There's no way I can jump! That waterfall never ends!" But the decision was made for me, and we jumped. At first, my mind was actually frozen in place for what felt like forever before we were free-falling. I didn't have that terrifying drop in my stomach that makes me panic, and there was no landing. I was just on solid ground out of nowhere.

One of the most incredible dreams I ever had happened while I was living in the Caribbean. In the dream, I was sitting beside myself having a wordless conversation with myself. When I looked at myself, I saw through the eyes of not just the two of me, but I was also behind my selves watching them interact. I saw it from all three perspectives, but then again, there had to be more of me to be aware of all my selves.

End of Excerpt

Yes, I wrote that while I was living in the Caribbean.

Excerpt from Book Two:

February 2017

Monday

It had always been a dream of mine to live in the Caribbean. I'm from somewhere cold, and I hate the brutal winters. Unfortunately, visiting the Caribbean is one thing; living there is completely different. There was no work to be found, so I left and went to another Caribbean country, which I truly loved.

I applied for work, but again, nothing panned out. What had I been expecting? I had no clue really. But I believe in taking chances to see what I can do. I was absolutely amazed at my ability to adapt to living in the Caribbean so easily, especially the last country I was in. I felt I belonged there. I lived there for a while, but ended up returning to my own country.

End of Excerpt

November 2018

Thursday

I am *dreading* looking for another job, *again*! Oh, listen to me whine and complain about my first-world problems! There are some people who are about to become homeless because of the economy, and I've not had to work for the past two weeks. I don't really have to look for a job for a few more weeks, if I so choose. I am just so tired of constantly having to start over because I haven't found where I feel comfortable, peaceful, and joyful. That's because those feelings are from the inside, not the outside. Of course, I know this.

Friday

I was looking out my balcony window when I saw a homeless man going through the garbage. I thought he would probably appreciate my bottles. When I yelled this to him, he told me to drop them from the balcony and he'd be back to pick them up. (They wouldn't break on the grass and leaves.) I went and got the bottles and thought he might like the oranges I refused to eat because of the skin. So, I got those also and ran back onto the balcony, and he was still going through the garbage bin. I dropped them, and he said thanks. I then thought of what else I would end up tossing and went back into the kitchen and looked in my fridge. I saw the hummus I'd bought but no longer wanted and a bunch of mini carrots I'd forgotten about. I wondered if the carrots were still edible and if he would want hummus and reminded myself that he was going through the garbage bin with his bare hands and his home was a shopping cart.

I tossed those two items off the balcony. A bit later, I checked if he'd taken everything (didn't want to leave my trash on the lawn), and there was nothing left. He'd taken everything. Just a few days ago, I was complaining about my first-world problems. He was more grateful for my garbage than I am for all that I have. I don't know how this homeless man became who he is now. We all have a story as to why we are currently living our lives the way we are.

Saturday

I love it when this happens! I ran into an old friend at the gym today. I hadn't seen her for years. What's funny is that I didn't notice her, I noticed her coat on the bench as I was bent down untying my running shoes:

Me (looking down): Excuse me, where did you get your coat?

Stranger: It's an old coat!

Me (finally looking at the person): But it's…*hey*!

Friend: Oh my god! How are you?

She'd belonged to the gym for years, and I'd been there for thirteen months. And never in that entire time had I ever seen her before today, nor her me! Meeting her was so wild because of all the things that had to have transpired for us to have met like that. Think about it: On Monday, I told my friend that I had a book I'd give her after Tuesday's yoga class. She loves reading just as much as I do! I changed my mind and told her Wednesday would be better. After our class, we chatted for about ten minutes. Then I went down to the locker room and washed my hands and water bottle. I then went to my locker section, started to change, and as I was taking my shoes off, you know the rest. I love it when things are aligned perfectly like that – it's fun to realize. We've arranged to have lunch. Thanks, Universe.

I have been applying for jobs since yesterday. I know I still have the wrong attitude, but I received a reply from one place: "I was impressed with your resume and would like to follow up with you." Thanks again, Universe. I needed that huge boost!

Sunday

Had lunch with that old friend today. She too marvelled at how the Universe aligned everything, for her, in order for us to meet: She awoke earlier than expected and decided to head out to exercise. But as she was approaching the gym's parking lot, she changed her mind and decided to do some shopping first. She left and came back to the gym a while later. She was closing her locker, ready to leave, when she heard: "Excuse me, where did you get that coat?" Brilliant!

November 2018

Monday

I'm still in awe of what happened last night, although I shouldn't doubt the Universe!

I have an interview tomorrow for what I know would be the perfect job. I won't tell you what makes it perfect until after my interview tomorrow. How did this (potentially) incredible opportunity come about? I was watching TV when I got a phone call from a coworker at that job I'd quit. He told me about a job available immediately and that he'd spoken to the person about me. I know, right? That's just so thoughtful!

Tuesday

I just got back from my interview, and I want this job! It would be perfect for me. I'd be working mostly from home! I've always wanted to create my own hours and work independently. That's even better than what I'd been imagining!

Monday

Today, I went for another interview for a different job. I really like this job too! But not as much as the other job.

Monday

I got the dream job. Picture the biggest smile on my face, and that doesn't even come *close* to how I feel! Thank you, Universe. I sent a thank you note to the other job, because in my heart, I knew I would have been offered the job. I'll be going for training tomorrow. I am beyond excited!

Thursday

Sure enough, I was offered that other job! I guess they didn't read my email. I was only able to be trained for a few hours on my dream job. I'm a quick learner, but still. Sigh. My excitement has turned into outright panic!

Friday

Recently, an old friend of mine died. The shock and sadness I feel are incredible. I've been in a tailspin ever since, and then I started the new job. I have not been feeling that well for a while.

Excerpt from Book Two:

June 2018

Friday

Yet another incredibly rich and powerful person has committed suicide: Kate Spade. Obviously, I have no idea what Kate Spade was going through, but from the outside looking in, she had it all, which meant nothing in the end. I feel so sorry for her young daughter and the traumas that have now been created for her.

Why do our thoughts bring us so far down that we can't find a way to get back up? What is it about ourselves that we just can't seem to love enough to want to live? Times get tough for all of us, without exception. Isn't that evident by now? It's such a challenge to not get lost in our own darkness. And nobody can even fathom how dark we can become because we keep it all to ourselves.

Friday

I just learned that Anthony Bourdain committed suicide. While his pain and suffering has ended, the pain of his young daughter has just begun.

From PsychCentral.com:

Ways You Can Help Your Child Quiet Their Negative Self-Talk

We all have an inner critic who feeds on negative self-talk, unkind, unsupportive words from others and criticism. While most of us have developed ways to cope with this harsh inner voice, kids and teens often lack the tools to effectively deal with it…. Left unchecked, the inner critic's voice can become so loud it drowns out everything else…. It might take a while to banish your child's inner critic, but the earlier you teach your kid to quit their negative self-talk, the better chance they'll have to live a happy and fulfilling life. (Tyler Jacobson. PsychCentral.com. 2018. "Ways You Can Help Your Child Quiet Their Negative Self-Talk." Last modified July 8. https://muckrack.com/tyler-jacobson/articles.)

While this article is focused on helping children, I think adults need just as much help with their negative self-talk. My inner critic is very loud with thoughts of hate, shame, fear, etc. No amount of treatment or medication can truly stop our torturous thoughts, unless we're willing to understand them, nor can anyone else in our lives (children or spouses) make us want to live – no matter how much we love them – because it's ourselves that we can't stand to be around.

I woke up this morning and practiced my positive affirmations and gratitude for all that I have. Then out of nowhere, I realized the significance this day has, and I started to feel so sad and depressed. More than a decade ago, my Mum entered her last few weeks of life. I started to ruminate on that entire experience – from the first day I started to care for her until the day she died. My mind started counting down how many days to go until she actually died, and I started crying.

On a lighter note, one of my yoga friends told me that during Savasana (resting pose) her mind had been wandering and not resting. She told me the thought that popped into her head during this silent time was, "It'd really hurt if you put your hand in boiling water." She had no idea where that thought even came from. She even gave herself the shivers picturing it, all while she was supposed to be relaxing and enjoying the stillness. We laughed at the absurdity of those horrible thoughts during a time of peace and tranquility. Our thoughts have a mind of their own. It takes so much skill and effort to not get lost in them.

End of Excerpt

December 2018

Tuesday

I am about to *break* for the third time.

I am so completely and utterly overwhelmed with my new job that I am losing it! I have to go into the office soon. It'll be my first time, and I'm scared! Not excited, but terrified. How am I going to be able to do this? Universe, what have you gotten me into? Breathe, Lee.

Today is Tuesday, and I'm stressing about something that will happen days from now. Why can't I remember how to live in the now? Why can't I have faith and trust in myself to know I'll do my absolute best when I go into the office? Why can't I feel confidence in myself? Why always panic, Universe? I guess I understand my *fear* better than I understand my *love*.

Wednesday

I am still so nervous.

We humans are so messed up! I have such a fear of my dreams coming true. How does that make sense? I have not let go of my solid false belief that I'm not worthy of my dreams. When I know what I'm doing and love what I do, I'm excellent at my job. Why do I constantly doubt my abilities?

Apropos of nothing, I'm tired of being ripped off. I always buy the same litter. Recently, I noticed it wasn't lasting as long as it usually did. I went to get more litter this past weekend, and sure enough, the amount in the litter bag had gone down several pounds, but it was still the same price. When I brought the bag up to the counter to pay for it, I asked the clerk if they expected to get the bigger bags anytime soon. The clerk said the brand had decreased its weight – but the price remained the same. So, I'm to pay the same price for less?

Later, I went to the bank to take out some money. I was told that if I took it out of my "other" account, I'd be charged five dollars. Charged for what, exactly? I was told my "other" account could only be withdrawn from online without penalties. Ridiculous!

Wednesday

I'm starting to get excited about tomorrow!

I really am enjoying this new job and, my goodness, to be able to watch the beginning of what's to be quite a mess of snow from the comfort of my Zen room is, simply, amazing! Thank you, Universe.

Friday

Well, I did it!

I had my first and second day at the office, and I survived! Of course, there were lots of little misadventures: The last place I worked had its label printer set up separately as an icon. When I went into the office, I didn't remember that the last print job was for a label. I arrived at the office early and needed to print twenty copies of a four-page document. So, I did. Except, as I mentioned above, it was still set to the label printer. Oops! Indeed! I frantically turned the label machine off and unplugged all the cables, but still, when I hooked everything back together and turned the label printer back on, out came label after label of my four-page document. I even tried watching the instructional video, but when the video came on, the sound on my computer had been turned up to the loudest setting. (Did I mention there were people sitting in the waiting area?) I didn't know where the volume control was on the computer, and I was in panic mode before I realized I could turn the volume down on the video. My boss came out of his office with a client and asked me to print a label. I'd been working for only twenty minutes at that point. Sigh. Later, I had to input all this information, which had to be done with two screens. Yes, I was shown how to do this, and I wrote very clear and specific notes on the process. But it didn't work. I even went so far as to call my trainer, but what could she say other than, "Just drag it over to the other screen." I would if I could!

Thankfully, the boss from the other business we share an office with came in (thanks, Universe!) and I asked her. She explained that the reason I couldn't drag the screen over to the second computer was because I had my first screen maximized. Huh? I hadn't been looking at whether the screen was maximized or not when I was being trained, as I was too busy taking copious notes. But it went well, and today went even better!

Another dream of mine is to be a professional student. I just love learning. Well, I've been given the opportunity with this job. It's evident that I'm going to have to teach myself to decipher the codes, learn the terminology, and understand the correct procedures. Most things I need to know can be found online, and I can always look through random client files to understand how my trainer did it. It's daunting, but I'm up for the challenge.

December 2018

Monday

I am so pissed off right now!

Last week, I helped someone out who was in a financial bind, and they told me they'd repay me yesterday. I went to collect my money and was told they needed three more weeks to repay me because it was almost Christmas, and they wanted to buy presents for their adult kids. I'm sorry, what? I didn't expect that from them. I told them that "as it was almost Christmas," I needed my money back to buy presents myself. Ok, so the presents were all for me, but whatever, you know? I was given my money back.

January 2019

Monday

I've still been living with frustration and anxiety. It's the job – there's just so much still that I'm learning, and the last time I was in the office, there was tons of work left to do. I decided to go in extra early – I've been going in an hour early just to get organized and get as much work done as possible before the clients arrive – so I planned to be there one and a half hours before I officially started my day.

We've been having extremely frigid weather recently, with lots of snow dumping in between. On Sunday, I was going to get a coffee, and my car was dead. I figured it was just the temperature, so I got my battery charger out and attempted to attach it, but it was dead too. I spent six hours charging the battery, but the car still wouldn't start. I kept trying and, eventually, the car started. I let it run for twenty minutes and then drove around the parking area, all the while looking at the message, "Engine Malfunction. Service Now!" with a picture of a wrench. Ok, then. I guess I'll be taking it in on Tuesday to be serviced. I was livid. I didn't have the extra money for any type of emergency, as I'd wasted it on absolute crap, which made me angry that I wasn't making enough money. The truth is, I have no idea what enough money is since I waste most of it. Later in the evening, I started the car a couple of times with my amazing remote starter (smartest investment ever), and it was fine.

I got up yesterday morning and tried to remote start the car – but nothing. I went out and hooked the charger back on. Still nothing. I started to panic. I realized I'd have to forget about it and get a taxi as I was going to be late if I wanted to be extra early to work. More money to spend – and I'd have to have the car towed to the garage now, which meant even more money required.

The taxi driver was commenting on how treacherous the roads were. I was feeling so upset about all the money and other things (my life) that the tears came. The taxi driver heard and saw me crying, so I said, "Things just aren't working out the way I want them to, and I'm tired of it all." He told me I had to brush it off, because other people had it much worse (such as whoever was in that accident we'd just passed). True, but so *not* helpful. He talked about being positive, and I told him that the Universe probably didn't want me driving. I'd wondered how I would have driven under the treacherous road conditions, being in such a rush and all.

The day went by, and after taking a taxi home, I visited SAF. I was just so angry about my day and the car not starting. I was allowed to wallow in negativity with SAF's own negativity. It was a party, let me tell you! We complained about everything being wrong in our lives for hours.

Tuesday

I got up to see if the booster would work, and it did! See? The Universe really didn't want me on the roads yesterday. I let the car run for twenty minutes, and then drove it around the block. I had to do something before I went to the garage, so I turned it off. When I went to drive to the garage, the car wouldn't start, again. I got the booster out again. Did I mention it was bitterly cold with blowing, freezing wind? This time, the car wouldn't start at all. I tried for probably twenty more minutes. I kept looking at cars, wondering why not one person slowed down to ask if I needed help when my car hood was up. I asked the Universe to please bring me someone to help, and the next car that drove by actually stopped. The man rolled down his window and just stared at me while I kept asking if he could help me. I'm embarrassed to say, but when he hadn't replied, but kept staring at me, I blurted out, "Stop staring!" I didn't like what that stare was telling me. He finally got out of his car, and I asked him, once again, if he could help me. He was kind of smiling at me, but in a strange way. He finally spoke. (The conversation was all in French. I impressed myself – seriously.):

Guy: You don't recognize me?

Me: No, but that means I probably should, right?

Guy: My face isn't familiar to you?

Me: No, not at all.

Guy: I'm friends with one of your neighbours.

Me: Oh. Um…well, it's really kind of you to stop. Can you please help me? You're very kind.

Guy: I'm a kind guy.

Me: Seriously, I can't believe this. I can't believe you're actually willing to help me. Please accept my apology for my previous behaviour. I'm truly sorry. And again, thank you so much for stopping to help me.

So, my neighbours. What to say? They've caused me problems since the day I moved in – noise problems. After many years of this, I had a chat with the authorities. Indeed, I did. Also, when I moved in, my neighbours' friends would always park in my spot (we have no visitors' parking), which made me furious, as I'd always have to knock on the neighbours' door and tell them their friends were in my spot, over and over again. I guess you could say I yelled at these visitors quite rudely for a time, until they stopped parking in my spot. Apparently, the guy helping me was one of the friends I'd yelled at. Oops! I brought my car to the garage to be looked at.

Wednesday

I got the call to pick the car up around 3:30 pm. The Uber arrived at 4:10 pm. Because of the road conditions – dangerous

– we got stuck in traffic because he took a route that had an accident on it. He even said he'd gone the wrong way, thinking the accident was further up the road. After sitting in traffic for twenty to thirty minutes, he finally did a U-turn, and we took an accident-free route, arriving at the garage at 5:00 pm when it should have taken us ten minutes. I was told the car was fine – just that the battery couldn't handle the cold. I've had the battery for only one and a half years. I live in a very cold country. Shouldn't the battery and car be able to handle the cold for goodness' sake?

Thursday

I checked my email messages, and the cost for the Uber ride was triple the price. Excuse me?

I went online and disputed the charge, explaining that the driver had taken a poor route. They instantly refunded me the extra, extra charges.

I've been spending so much time with SAF, and I'm beginning to understand that this might not be such a good idea. Why? It's a case of misery loves company. We do laugh and whatnot, but our time together is unhealthy with our own ways of numbing our pain. I'm just so tired of feeling alone. I have no problem being by myself, but after a while, I miss talking and hanging out, you know?

I've received so many compliments from the clients at work on being so pleasant and helpful and understanding. This is totally new for me! It's such a wonderful feeling when you receive that genuine, brief connection. One guy liked me so much that he asked me out on Monday when we were in the office. At first, I said yes. I was so flattered. Yah, that's sad. But I really didn't want to be bothered with someone I honestly wasn't interested in. Then why say yes in the first place? Sigh. The next day when he called me to chat, I told him I had to cancel because the guy I'd been semi-dating asked me to get serious, so it'd be wrong for him and me to meet for coffee. If I'd said no right away, I wouldn't have had to lie and make up a non-existent boyfriend. Of course, the guy understood. And then he ruined it by asking me if I had any friends who'd be interested in having coffee with him. Whatever!

Monday

So yesterday, I cried most of the day. Why? When I say I am alone, it's because I have no family. It's because my experience is that I have no family. I look to my friends for support, except recently, they're letting me down. If I don't check in with them, I don't hear from them, so I stopped calling, emailing, and texting most of them. And guess what? Not a peep from anyone. Is it so hard to send a quick one-line text saying, "Hey, how goes?" One friend hasn't reached out since the beginning of December. We are all busy, but it can't always be only one person keeping the communication going. If I were to send this one particular friend a text, I'd get a response immediately. It hurts my heart always being the one to reach out – it feels like I've been forgotten.

Tuesday

Lately, I've been having the most intense, incredible, vivid dreams. When I wake up, I start thinking about how phenomenally detailed they are and the switches from one scene to something completely different. It's mesmerizing, all the little details that have been culled from my day or whenever they are being remembered from. The intricacies shocked me, and I thought,

"I am so brilliantly creative!" And it's true. I subconsciously created wonderment and terror. Let's be real about dreams – fear will penetrate everywhere. But I created it all.

And then from nowhere, I remembered Deepak Chopra speaking of this in his book *Power Freedom and Grace – Living from the Source of Lasting Happiness*:

> One night I dreamed I was playing golf and won a trophy. There were a hundred people in the gallery, and they all cheered when I got this beautiful trophy. The next day my photo was in the newspaper. Then I woke up and said, "Oh my God, I made up the whole thing. I was Deepak who won the trophy. I was the golf course, I was the hundred people, and I was the photo in the newspaper". But I didn't know that when I was dreaming; I only knew it when I woke up. (Chopra, 2008)

February 2019

Thursday

Just received an email from one of my friends who's been silent. This friend wrote, "It's been *way* too long." And I thought, "It's been as long as you needed to remember that I'm not the only person in this friendship."

Monday

The other day, a friend told me that she'd never been in love. I told my friend that I, too, had never been in love. She guessed there were probably so many more people in the world who'd never found that one special love, but that society made it seem otherwise. Instead of focusing on marrying and settling down with that one special person as the purpose of life, maybe we should first start with self-love as the most important purpose. So that's exactly what I'm going to do for myself!

Saturday

The Universe is trying to remind me of something very important.

Last night I had one of my strange recurring dreams that involved two people from my distant past. John was someone I'd wanted to spend my life with (but the feeling wasn't returned) and Jane was a good friend at one point in my life. It's been more than a dozen years since I last saw John and Jane. John and Jane met once when we all went out together one night, and they never saw each other again after that one night.

In my dream, I'm hanging out with my friend Jack in some house that's having a party, when suddenly John appears. I am so happy to see John, and the three of us chill together in our own corner. Jane stops by with some of her friends, and we're having a great time until I see Jane start to flirt with John. I'm so angry at Jane for doing this to me, but I have faith in John to not respond to her obvious games. Unfortunately, John does respond, and I see the two of them go off together into the bedroom. Jack's doing all he can to distract me and tell me not to be friends with either of them anymore and that we should leave, but I am so enraged and jealous that I refuse to leave. After a while, I see John and Jane emerge from the bedroom with bathrobes on.

And then I wake up.

I created something that never happened – and that's exactly what fears and worry do. I hadn't had that dream for a year maybe. I honestly don't remember. But in the past when

I've woken up from it, my first thought has always been, "Why the hell won't John and Jane stay out of my dreams?" And then I'd start thinking about them and wonder why I made something up that never happened, without really thinking about the why did I make that up. I believe I had that dream after reading that passage from Deepak Chopra's book. It's all about our thoughts and what we make up. I was able to turn a one-time encounter between John and Jane that happened more than a decade ago, and was innocent, into a betrayal that causes me so much pain today. The Universe is reminding me of the power of my thoughts to create events, real or false.

Tuesday

I just want someone to tell me: "You're an amazingly beautiful being – *so* worth loving." I know I'm the only one who can tell that to myself. And, damn it, SAF stopped by yesterday because she brought me something. I could have said no, of course, but I kind of wanted what she was bringing – nothing unhealthy. But then it turned into an unhealthy evening. Sigh. What are you doing Lee? You're wasting all your money, you're unhappy, you want to change everything about yourself and…I'm really in a mood right now.

It's maddening when a specific date arrives, and it has an effect on you that you're trying to deny. I wasn't initially thinking of Valentine's Day, but might as well admit that I'm bothered that no one will be calling *me* to say they love me. And I know it's all my own doing, but whatever.

It's another date I'm thinking about. At times, it's overwhelming to live your truth. There are several dates that I've got to learn not to attach any meaning to.

You know how I keep saying there are no coincidences? I hurt my back on Saturday – not sure how – but then I aggravated it even more by tensing it as I was carrying something heavy over an icy and very lumpy path. I couldn't do the one thing I do really love: Yoga. It's just the tension I've been holding in my body.

My attitude towards work has soured, and that needs to change immediately! It's terrible how easy it is to stop seeing how wonderful something truly is and allow it to become something of a chore. Due to my inattention regarding my job, I made some future mistakes that would have become frustrating and annoying for others had the Universe not stepped in and allowed me to see them in the present. I remember being at my job in the other country for over a year, when my boss asked me, "Do you not like working here or want to be here anymore?" The boss had said this after I stopped caring and was making lots of mistakes. That smartened me up very quickly. Smarten up, Lee.

Thursday

So, today's Valentine's Day.

On this day of *love*, Lee, I thank you for taking the time to remember who you are without all the noise of people who don't have your best interests at heart. Only you do, Lee.

Monday

I am absolutely *mortified* to share this with you, but I want to get a point across. (Don't forget, these are only my beliefs.) I've been praying, wishing, hoping that when I select a Tarot card, it'll be the Magician. Why? Because the Magician is magical and miraculous. Why should I be wishing, praying, hoping for some card to remind me of who I truly am, and then magically, when this card's chosen, all will be well and I'll start loving myself? Oy vey! That's just grasping, Lee. You don't need a card to tell you how powerful you truly are.

Tuesday

I know you'll never believe this, but it's the absolute truth!

When I pulled my Tarot card before going to bed tonight, I pulled the Magician. I burst out laughing! As if! But it was right there in my hand. So? Is all well, and do you now love yourself Lee? Of course not!

I've hurt my back. It's the stress I'm feeling about going into the office tomorrow. I have started having panic attacks again. We are becoming way too busy. I recall my boss saying he wasn't sure he liked how busy he was becoming – said it was a bit much.

Thursday

I am supposed to be loving awareness.

There's a couple in my neighbourhood who must not have winter tires on because after every snowfall, their car gets stuck in the exact same spot they park in every single day. They rev the car back and forth for around twenty minutes getting nowhere, but making lots of noise. They must also not have a shovel because they just kick the snow out of the way. I've listened and watched on several occasions and seen strangers helping this couple by putting mats down and pushing from behind. And eventually, with all this help they get unstuck and head out, only to return to the same spot.

Tonight, they finally called a tow truck after no one arrived to their aid. I wonder where they'll park when they return. Universe? I am lovingly aware that these two are stupid idiots. This is the stuff I'm supposed to wash off my back and not let disturb me? Yes, Lee.

Friday

Oh, Lee! Why are you even thinking about this? SAF went on holidays and will be back this weekend, and I've been getting annoyed at myself knowing we'll get together. I thought you were done with SAF? I did too. But it's hard when you're lonely and want company. Any company is better than no company, right? No, not right. In fact, very wrong, Lee. Sigh.

Please work on your patience, Lee. The right people will be brought to you in due time. Universe, I am asking you to please help me with my patience. Um... Universe? Hello? I want to be patient now!

Addendum – I'd shut the computer down forty-five minutes ago. Fifteen minutes ago, I got a message from SAF. "I'm back." Universe? I really don't appreciate your sense of humour!

Saturday

Of course, I disappointed myself and saw SAF. The calls wouldn't stop. Why I couldn't ignore them speaks to my weaknesses. I am lovingly aware that I, too, am a stupid idiot! I think I've learned all I need to know about myself: I am a creature of bad habits.

March 2019

Saturday

What an incredibly stressful week! And I'm still carrying so much stress in my body. It's all work-related. Sigh. At one point I even thought about quitting. No, not again, Lee. So much for my dream job, eh? Why am I spending all my time stressing over work?

Sunday

Why am I spending all my time stressing over work? Yes, why am I? This is not how I envisioned my dream job. Working from home is a dream, but that's about it. I am not happy. It's just way too stressful. The pace of work is not what my mind or body can handle. I was going to give it a few months, to see if that helped, but it's not like my boss is going to get less busy. If anything, he'll become even busier. I am more important than any job.

Saturday

I called a friend and kind of broke down. I was so embarrassed! The reality of quitting another job due to stress has me stressed, and that's not right. Will I ever find a job that's reasonable? There is only so much a person can, but more importantly, should do. This new world of working nonstop is so stressful and not how I want to live my life.

I went to the doctor yesterday to up my meds. Yes, this is how stressed I've been. I went somewhere and ran into someone I hadn't seen for years. I saw her first, and my immediate reaction was to hide! But then I remembered the good times we had, and when she finally turned and saw me, I had a big grin on my face. She seemed genuinely happy to see me. I have some very difficult emotions regarding this person. And yet, it really was great to run into her once I relaxed. Since there are no coincidences, it's pretty incredible all the little and big things that had to transpire for us to meet.

Friday

I spoke with someone who said I shouldn't quit my job just yet, but to give it a few more months. Another friend called, and she gave me so much support and encouragement. She, too, told me not to quit.

Sunday

I have been wracked with doubt about whether I should stay or quit. And that, of course, is creating more stress than necessary. I believed it was my dream job because I could work from home. Another change? So soon? What do you want me to do, Universe? Work or not work?

Am I really ready to throw caution to the wind, jump, and have you catch me? Um… Lee? Isn't that what you're trying to help others understand – how to be their own magician? But what if I waste my time like I've done every other time I've taken a break and then had to scramble to find a job so that I have money to pay the bills? Yes, that is my cycle of insanity.

Monday

I don't understand the college admissions bribery scandal. Why do it? Why pay hundreds of thousands of dollars so that your teenager can go to an elite college or university that they don't qualify for? Does a fake degree really mean something? Why is it so hard to be honest? Why not let your child do what they're truly capable of and what they'd really like to do? Why try to buy your dreams for somebody else? How is any of that love?

Wednesday

I am absolutely in turmoil over this bloody job! My hours had been increased, and I just got my new paycheque. I started thinking how awesome this new salary would be on a regular basis.

My thoughts ran like this: Is the job *so* bad? You really haven't given it a chance, and this week's been so calm – even though you've not had a break yet, and you're dreading going into the office next week. But is all that so horrible with this nice new paycheque? And you'll be asking for a raise in the summer so you'll be receiving an even *bigger* paycheque! Money, money, money! I'll have it, but I know I won't be happy. The fight within me is real. I should work! No, I should remember who I truly am.

"But how will I survive, Universe?"

"Do you have money in your account, Lee?"

"Yes."

"Enough to live on for a year, if necessary?"

"Yes, but no money will be coming in, and then what?"

"Are your mind, body, and spirit living in peace and harmony when you are working, Lee?"

"No."

"What was the question again, Lee?"

Friday

For the past two nights I've woken up several times and not been able to get back to sleep. I can't believe how nervous I am to quit.

Monday

So, it's done. I've officially quit my job!

Friday

I haven't slept properly for two nights now. It's amazing how other people's opinions can have you doubting yourself. Two different people told me about options for staying at my job that I'd never even considered. Lee? I thought your mind was made up. It was, but then someone I talked to had a completely different take on the situation, which made me think about trying the idea. But I won't waver again. I really hope I can get a good night's rest now.

Last night I dreamt that I was at this futuristic structure for a convention centre. It was so cool because there were different levels and glass buildings within this massive structure. There were so many events taking place all at once, and I seemed to float from one to another. Sometimes I knew nobody in the room, yet I was always welcomed. I had to go to the loo, and when I opened the door to go in, there was a man inside waiting for his girlfriend, who was in an ornately carved wooden structure. I stood beside the man and waited. When the girlfriend came out, the man said to his girlfriend, "I'm going to toss these golden coins up in the air. See how many you can collect until I tell you to stop." I knew it was a game they always played. The loo's floor had the most beautiful gold mosaic design. I asked if I could play too, and he said, "Of course!" And he tossed loads of gold coins in the air, and when they landed, I dove and grabbed as many as I could. Because everything was gold, a silver engagement ring caught my eye, and I picked it up quickly. I looked to see if his girlfriend had noticed, but as I watched her, I noticed she wasn't looking down to see the coins. She was using her hands to feel where they were, yet she wasn't blind. I looked back to the guy, but he wasn't watching me either; he was transfixed by his girlfriend. I opened my hand and looked at the ring shining amongst all that gold and thought, "I found it. It's mine. That's not nice, Lee. You should give it back as they allowed you to grab so many gold coins. But I found it, it should be mine." Then I was in another room, still holding the ring in my palm when I saw the couple again, and she was fawning over this beautiful gold ring she'd found. I felt such guilt for secretly hiding the silver ring that I went up to them and gave it back. I'm not a dream interpreter, but I think there's a lot of symbolism in that dream.

April 2019

Thursday

The game of telephone is alive and well! I told fewer than five people exactly why I was leaving – always stressing that my boss was the easiest to work for, which is the truth, but that the job was way too busy for me (again, the truth).

Yesterday, I went into the office. The new people who took over our station (we're moving locations) were in as well. They have two administrators working in the office, and I spoke with one of them last week for five minutes, saying nothing about me leaving. Today, they both told me they'd heard I was quitting. The one I met for the first time yesterday told me she'd heard that I'd quit because I'd asked my boss to work full-time and he'd said no, it was only a part-time job. Can someone explain to me how these two strangers heard false rumours about me? Unbelievable!

Saturday

My replacement has been hired! I can't tell you how relieved I feel because I'm still stressing.

One of the many challenging lessons I've yet to master is that I can't run away from the past. Yet, try I do, mightily.

Last night, I dreamt about my molester. Man, I'm so tired of that occurring! In the dream, I was being forced to accept and love this person, and I didn't know how to. But more importantly, I didn't want to. What brought the dream on? I'd told an old friend about a picture I had of the two of us when we were seven or eight that I would post on Facebook once I found it. I went through photo album after photo album to find it. Seeing the little me in the pictures from when I was six onwards hurt. I could see and feel my discomfort in certain pictures. And then, the other day, I learned news of someone whom I'll never see again because of my speaking up and out about being abused.

So, I started down the road of *I've got to get out of this area.* Must I? Right now, I don't know, but the instinct to run is strong. But then that's always been my M.O., and the hurt still finds me no matter the distance. I started crying. I told my child-self how sorry I was for what happened to her. And I am. And that's the hurt I must stop running from.

Oh! I went to pick up my meds, and it went like this:

Pharmacist: We don't have your brand at the moment. This is the generic kind. They should work the same.

Me: They *should* or they *will* work the same?

Pharmacist: They *should*.

Me: Well, how will I know if they're not working as well?

Pharmacist: If you have mood changes…

No. No thank you. The last thing I need right now is a mood change on top of my panic and stress. Thankfully, they had enough to give me until the shipment arrives Monday.

Sunday

The Tarot card I chose this morning talked about releasing grief, forgiveness, and honouring my emotions. I talked to a friend in order to vent it out. I was talking about my job, and she said, "When you say those things, those are signs of being burnt out." I replied, "I've long since been burnt out – there are not even any fumes remaining." I've got to heal my past. That's where my burnout comes from.

Thursday

Someone told me an absolutely disgusting story of being betrayed. Silently, I questioned this person's sanity at still holding out hope for a reconciliation. How could this person still even be entertaining such a revolting thought? Let it go! Think better of yourself! *Love* yourself!

Yes, Lee. It made me realize that I, too, have been holding out hope.

My experience is that everyone has moved on. I feel as though I'm the only one who's stuck. I've been in denial. Where I once had a seat at the table, I feel my seat no longer exists. Yet, I do.

That's hard for my head and heart to come to terms with. That's why I am so tired. Yet, I created that specifically so that I could be free to remember who I truly am. Be careful what you wish for.

Thursday

I'm kind of shocked by what I did!

I've put away the pictures of my Mum and Dad. Why did I do that, you ask? I will always love my Mum and Dad, but I'd kind of created this shrine to both of them that I no longer need. They are with me regardless of any pictures on my walls. This is the time for me to completely let go of the past without any guilt or shame. I kept my inconvenient reality buried for them. I believe, in my heart, it would have destroyed my Mum had I forced her to talk about my being abused. But both my parents passed over a decade ago. I don't want or need to be wondering what they think of the stand I've taken with the family. I'm not a bad girl, nor am I in trouble for wanting to be free. I have to believe they are proud of me for being true to myself. I am free to create me.

Friday

So that's it then!

I returned my very last phone call, booked my very last appointment, confirmed my last meeting, created the last client profile I'll ever have to learn about and packed up the computer for the last time as it's an office day on Monday. I still have to shadow on Monday, but I'm not doing any work. This is his show now.

Sunday

It's incredible all the endings that have happened recently. I am actually getting excited about tomorrow! When I come home tomorrow night, the crazy work calendar will no longer constantly be in my view. (I'm generously giving it to him, and I can, finally, have my Zen room back! Man, I am so grateful, Universe.)

I won two tickets to a concert that happened last night. My friend and I went to get a drink. After I paid for my beer and went to take it from the cashier, he opened the beer before I could say anything.

Me: I didn't want my beer opened now.

Cashier: It's our policy.

Me: That doesn't make sense. I didn't want to have to carry an open can of beer around.

Cashier: Sorry, but it's our policy to open them.

I didn't even bother engaging because two seconds ago I'd been happy. But, seriously? That's an incredibly stupid policy. We're at a concert with tons of people bumping into each other. I'll be lucky if there's any beer left once we get back to our seats. We had such a good time at the concert! I hadn't been to one in more than a decade.

Monday

I just finished my last office day!

May 2019

Sunday

Ok, lots to get caught up on.

It took me most of Tuesday to realize that I am no longer working! I must have checked my phone for messages at least four times throughout the day. But I had the best day. I went shopping and then took myself to the movies (cheap Tuesday), which I hadn't done in months.

I decided to book a trip! One week from today, I'll be on my way to the Caribbean! So excited!

Yesterday, I had the most incredible encounter with a stranger. I went to a box store (to buy a box), and the sales guy asked me why I was so happy. He even pretended to call the police because he'd never encountered someone so happy! We started talking, and I told him I'd quit my job, and he said, "I am so sorry for what you went through." The thing was, I didn't tell him what I experienced. He said my entire demeanor changed when I talked about my job, and he could see the toll it had taken on me. He gently asked if he could give me a hug, and I said yes! I started to tear up because here was a stranger who really saw me. He told me I had a beautiful smile, but explained it wasn't just my smile, but that it was my spirit that shone through. He felt I was a genuine person and thanked me for the brief connection we shared that day. Thank you, Universe, for that experience.

I spent the rest of yesterday spring cleaning. A total of four garbage bags left my place. It feels wonderful to have purged. I was going to throw out most of my photo albums, but I didn't want to look at them. I'll deal with them another time.

Tuesday

I can't believe my trip to the Caribbean has already come and gone! There were times when I couldn't wait to be home. And now, naturally, I wish I could go back! Why is it so hard to be happy where you are when you're there?

It was a very strange trip! The hotel was horrible! Ok, let me correct that. The actual rooms were fine, but there was no beach. And, for me, this was supposed to be a beach vacation. They called it a man-made beach, which took less than two minutes to swim the length of. Uh huh. No, not happy. So, there were a lot of very disappointed and frustrated guests, myself included. One couple arrived and waited on the beach as their agent found them another hotel. Their confirmation clearly specified a beachfront room. Because I'd booked this trip so last minute, I had to take an island view. Still, the advertising of the beach was very misleading online.

But the sun was hot, I enjoyed the food, and I met some really nice people. Of course, there was one idiot couple, naturally. Sigh. We'd been on the same flight down, and on the bus ride to the hotel, the husband caused an issue because he had to smoke! When the driver dropped off the passengers at another hotel, the driver opened the bus door on the right and got out, and so did the passengers for this hotel, along with Mr. Smoker. While the driver was unloading the luggage, Mr. Smoker lit up, away from the open bus door. The driver returned to the bus, entering on the left side, closed the door on the right side, and started to drive away. Mr. Smoker ran to the door and started banging on it, while Mrs. Smoker cried out from behind me, "My husband's outside!" The driver stopped and let Mr. Smoker back on. Mr. Smoker huffed and laughed with the driver saying, "I went out to have a cigarette, and I thought you'd be coming back from this side! I didn't see you! I didn't know there was another door on that side." He was laughing again as he sat down behind me. Idiot.

Naturally, Mr. and Mrs. Smoker were staying at the same hotel as I was. At the hotel, he started screaming and cursing while checking in because he'd believed his room had a balcony (in order to smoke). Yes, that was pleasant. But honestly? I was pissed too because I also needed a balcony. I've never been in a resort that didn't have balconies or patios. So, I paid a ridiculous amount for a bloody balcony!

Anyway, back to the idiot. Which idiot, Lee? You or him? Sigh. I was lying on a beach chair, staring out at the non-beach with the depressing view in front of me when I saw Mr. and Mrs. Smoker start to walk into the water, and he was puffing on his cigarette! I actually said out loud, "Oh! My! God!" and I stood up. There was a man sitting up, and I went to him and pointed out the idiot smoking in the ocean and said we had to do something! He told me to tell the lifeguards and let them handle it. Smart advice. I was just so outraged! Smoke all you want, but not in the ocean! I'm still outraged to be honest.

After I got the lifeguards, I went back and talked with the man who was still sitting up. I'd hoped he too would be single, but he was there with his wife, so the three of us spent time together.

It truly is a small world! They'd come from the exact same city in that other country I'd lived in! They told me how much the area I'd lived in had changed and become extremely expensive.

When I left, rent for the beautiful one-bedroom apartment I was living in was around $950.00. I'm not exactly sure, but I know it was close to that. We looked up the current rent, and my jaw dropped! It's now renting for $3750.00. That's almost a 300% increase in a decade! That's insane!

Friday

I wish I could let other people's actions not affect me, but they do. Remember me mentioning the problems I had with the neighbour whose friends always parked in my spot? I bought flowers for my deck. (I got way fewer this year, as I'm finally understanding that plants need space to grow. Don't we all?) I was out on my balcony enjoying the beautiful sun and potting the flowers, when this neighbour, let's call him Mr. FDB, pulled into his parking spot. We looked at each other when he exited his car. He went to the back seat of his car and removed a large plastic garbage bag, closed his car door, and dumped his trash on the grass, walking by the enormous garbage bin. Yes, he dumped his garbage on the grass!

The next morning, before leaving for yoga, I picked up the trash bag from the grass and put it on the trunk of Mr. FDB's car. We leave at somewhat the same time. Sure enough, Mr. FDB turned the corner and started walking to his car and sort of stopped, looking at his car. He got into his car, with me watching him, and drove off with the trash bag still on the trunk! He turned left, away from the parking exit, and drove off. He must have tossed the trash bag somewhere else, because when he returned and was passing my car towards the exit, the trash bag was gone!

I sat there and thought about what I'd just done – that from the moment I'd woken up, Mr. FDB's actions from the day before had been on my mind and that I needed to retaliate.

On Monday, I gave notice to vacate – not a moment too soon, apparently. I have until September to find somewhere to create my new beginning.

June 2019

Sunday

Oh, Universe! I am absolutely *terrified*! What have I done? I have no idea where I'm going to move to, and that's creating so much stress within my body. I hurt my back when I had my tires changed. Instead of lifting them one at a time, I picked up two at a time. And the next day, my neck, shoulders, and back were hurting. But it's now Sunday, and my neck, shoulders, and back are still so tense, like there's a vice turning and tightening them. That's stress – stress of not knowing where I'm going to live. I know I need to leave, but always in the past, I had a direction. Not this time.

I don't want to work wherever it is I land, but what if I do need to find something part-time? Will there be jobs? Will I get hired? What's going to happen to me? These are my fears, which are cycling through my mind non-stop. Why did I need to move again?

I spoke with a friend today, and our conversation has me upset. I know most people don't truly understand adoption unless they've experienced it, but I wish they wouldn't say, "Well, your family isn't even really your blood anyway." For me, that statement feels like a jab to my heart, and I wince each time I hear it (and I've heard it a lot). My family was just as real a family for me as yours. Blood has nothing to do with it. Why can't people open their minds and understand this?

Monday

I've just had the craziest, most insane experience!

I was sitting on my balcony. I'd been watching this man try to get his moped started, but the battery was dead. He walked his bike onto our property and started walking it along the grassy area in front of our parking lot. I asked him why he was walking his bike on the grass. (Why, Lee?) He told me to bleep-off. I told him he was on private property and to get off the grass. He continued to swear at me, and then plugged his moped into an electrical outlet from our building.

Did I mention he had a beer in his hand? His girlfriend (strung out on something) came over with a beer in her hand upon hearing her boyfriend yelling, and she too started swearing at me. The next part has to be censored, but the police were called (not by me). The policeman checked for outstanding warrants on the couple (none) and then told the couple they were on private property and had to leave. The couple left, as did the policeman.

No sooner than ten minutes later, the couple was back, but this time they were cursing and screaming at each other! The man was now on a bicycle and was trying to run his girlfriend down. He called her a crack-whore and said that he was going to kill her. She told him she was going to kill him. Someone in the area called the cops (again) because the same policeman came back. (I'd remembered the number on the hood of his car.) I ended up talking to the policeman (can't say why). We actually had the most fascinating conversation. Even though he was aware that the couple was extremely intoxicated, he couldn't arrest them. I don't understand why. The couple is known to the cops. (The cop said they were both on some heavy drugs – Fentanyl.)

In the midst of this mind-boggling conversation, I realized that there was a couple coming our way, and the guy was taking pictures of me with the cop. The couple stopped beside us and took more pictures. I asked the guy why he was taking our picture, and he told me about his rights. I asked him what he was hoping to accomplish by taking my picture with the cop. I also told the guy I hadn't consented to having my picture taken. The guy spouted more nonsense about his rights while he was taking a picture of the cop's license plate. Again, the cop said there was absolutely nothing he could do about the couple taking our pictures. Again, I don't understand why, as I specifically told the guy I didn't want my picture taken. The couple finally left. The cop said the guy taking the pictures would "probably post them online with the caption 'Cop Spotted Harassing Black Female' or 'Cop Seen Trying to Proposition Black Female.' It happens all the time." I could go on, but I think that's enough of that incredible ugliness!

Sunday

Happy Father's Day, Dad. I've been crying, of course. I've got to, somehow, let go of the guilt I carry within for not knowing you. What a shame we were both so stubborn.

Monday

Almost two months ago, I was able to buy a stereo unit that played my old iPod. (I hadn't listened to it since I moved to the Caribbean.) I came across the song "100 Years" by Five for Fighting. Oh man, do I ever love the piano in that tune, so much so that I'd ordered the sheet music and was teaching myself to play the song. Yes, I played the piano really well, once upon a time. I got rid of my piano when I moved to the Caribbean and never thought about it upon my return until I found that old iPod. I started to want a piano again. On Friday, I looked online to see if there were used digital pianos at a reasonable price, and I found one. The woman selling it said it'd only been used for eight months as her son no longer wanted to play the piano. I replied to the ad but figured it'd probably already been sold. Didn't hear back on Friday and had to tell myself on Saturday that it'd been snatched up and another piano would become available that I was meant to get. And then I got a message from the woman asking if I was still interested in buying it! I replied yes, we met, and I now have my piano! She told me she'd had other replies, but that mine stood out because it was heartfelt. She told me she was giving it to me with love and could feel the love I had for playing. Thanks, Universe!

July 2019

Tuesday

Today, I went to the gym and did a new class. I loved it! I was so enthusiastic too – everyone else was doing the class at a lower intensity than me. That doesn't matter one bit, but I find it funny when people take the time to exercise but do so grudgingly. There was nary a smile on anyone's face, and the teacher even said, "Come on! Smile everyone." I had the biggest grin on my face.

I'm going to spend the rest of the day cleaning, and then I'll do some reading and enjoy the fact that I'm not working but am focusing on myself. I'm feeling wonderful!

7:19 pm

That wonderful feeling has gone! I started to get so bloody angry! I wanted to rage. I even had to talk myself out of yelling at some idiot who was parked in the middle of the two-way street as I looked out my window while doing my dishes. The conversation in my head went like this: "Why is he parked there? And why is that other guy just leaning against the car? They *can't* park there! They're in the middle of the bloody road! What a bunch of idiots! Why are people so bleepin' ignorant? God, I hate people!" And then some other moron came out of the building holding some running shoes and walked to the guy leaning against the car. The car-leaner started to examine them, so my thoughts started again: "So they're selling shoes in the middle of the street? Are you bleeping kidding me?" And that's when I told myself to walk away. The dishes could wait. The anger is intense, and I know from where it stems. I'm forcing myself to be continuously silent in the company of someone who brings up a name that literally makes me stiffen and freezes me inside. So, stop seeing this person, Lee! I mean, really, how hard could it be? Much harder than I imagined.

August 2019

Thursday

It was definitely much harder than I imagined, but I did what I had to do. For me it's about respect. Whether you believe me or don't believe me that I was molested, do not bring up my molester's name to me. Ever. Is that really so hard? Yes, for some, apparently it is. And that's not my problem anymore.

4:08 pm

Oh man. I was in the grocery store's parking lot, having run into a neighbour. In the middle of our pleasant conversation, I heard a very loud voice.

Dolly (yelling): HEY, LEE!

Me: Oh, hi!

I continued my conversation with my neighbour and thought Dolly would walk on, but she didn't. She'd turned to face me.

Dolly (yelling even louder): I MADE YOU THAT THING, AND YOU NEVER TALKED TO ME AGAIN!

Me (sighing): Ok.

Dolly (yelling): I MADE YOU THAT THING, AND YOU NEVER TALKED TO ME AGAIN! THAT WAS REAL NICE OF YOU, LEE!

Me: Ok.

Dolly (yelling): I HAD YOU OVER, AND I MADE YOU THAT THING, AND YOU NEVER TALKED TO ME AGAIN! HOW COULD YOU DO THAT?

Me: Ok.

Dolly (yelling): I HOPE YOUR BOOK IS GREAT, AS YOU ONLY CARE ABOUT THE FAME AND FORTUNE! YOU'RE A REAL BITCH, LEE!

Me: Thank you.

And Dolly walked off. I knew this day would come. Dolly was absolutely correct. After she gave me that thing – more than ten months ago – I never acknowledged her again. So why didn't I ever talk to her again? When I first got to know Dolly, she told me a lot about herself that I believed. We'd see each other on the street or at the bus stop and chat our heads off. She spotted me one day and told me she had a painting for me, so I went to her place to get it. And that's when I realized a lot that she said wasn't true and made no sense, so I started going out of my way to avoid her. I hadn't seen her in months when we ran into each other as I was exiting my car. Dolly told me she'd made me something and wanted me to go with her to her place. So, I did. I know I shouldn't have, but I went because she seemed so lonely. What she'd made was edible. But she'd kept it in the *bathroom*, under the sink's cupboard, uncovered. No, no thank you. The thing never even made it home. I tossed it into the first garbage bin I saw.

But she's still a being with feelings. How should I have handled it? I could have continually made excuses every time I saw her, but that gets old. I could have just told her I was too busy, but I didn't want to have to talk to her again, ever. Actually, I should have stopped all communication the moment I understood what was going on, but I didn't, as I felt sorry for her. In the end, I hurt her more deeply than if I'd been honest.

Friday

I'm still feeling the hate and hurt directed towards me from Dolly, and I don't like the feeling at all.

Monday

It's been an emotional weekend.

I thought I'd feel better after letting that last person go, but instead my heart's hurting even more now that it's done. And Dolly's reckoning with me still hurts.

That specific therapist I saw specialized in sexual abuse. She told me something that pops into my head frequently. She said, "You can die of a broken heart." Gee, thanks! I mean, why would she say that? Of course, what she said is true, and that's the problem.

Wednesday

Yesterday, I drove to the new city I was thinking about moving to in order to view some apartments. Wow! What a disaster that was! Went to three different places, and they were nowhere near as big or as bright as my current place, and they were more expensive to boot.

It's so humbling having to admit that I'm in denial. I know I'm still trying to run away from the pain. Will it never end? I will be another year older soon and don't want to spend any more of my life running from my tormenting past. I will only be able to leave this area once I'm no longer bound to those who make me feel bad about myself for telling my truth.

Since I did what I had to do last week, my neck and left shoulder have been in a vice-like grip. The pain is terrible. There's so much pain inside of me that it's coming out through my body. Oh! My jaw is so tense as well. Fun times.

I have to change the beliefs I grew up with and stop believing that I am still a bad girl for no longer being silent. I'm not guilty, yet feel incredibly so. That's not right or fair. That's definitely not loving to myself.

These are the thoughts that are going through my head: Do I unfriend that person since we're no longer speaking? Do I get rid of the photo albums of my past since they're no longer real for me? Did my Mum really love me? Why didn't I speak up years ago? There are *so many* different emotions swelling and swerving inside of me! So yes, I do want to run away from them. It's the complete abandonment that I feel that's shocking and overwhelming to accept.

Friday

Today is the anniversary of my Mum's death.

I remember it like it was yesterday. I got the call early in the morning that she'd passed away after midnight. The place let me have a good night's sleep before dawn arrived, and I woke to a new reality. Mum? How does it make you feel to see me sitting alone at my own table now? I have no shame to carry. I was molested. I have to be comfortable saying that. I don't have to constantly be terrified all the time or feel that I'm in big trouble and will be punished for speaking my truth. Oh, Mum! I miss you!

Monday

I read a story about the ongoing issues of sexual abuse by priests. Why can't the Pope go on TV and profusely apologize for all the sexual abuse millions have suffered and continue to suffer from his men of God? Why continue to skirt the issue? It's a known fact. It feels as though the Pope is running away from facing this disgusting reality. They say "knowledge is power." The Pope has the "knowledge," and yet it appears there is a refusal to use his "power" to stop it.

What the Pope (and non-abused people) will never understand is the shame and guilt (among many other emotions) that live within the victim decades after the actual abuse.

Wednesday

Last Wednesday, I ran into one of my gym instructors. She gave me a big hug and asked where I'd been, as I was at the gym but hadn't taken her class. I'd arranged coffee with a friend. I told her I hurt my neck due to stress. She said she was going to make something for me. I got her beautiful gift today before class – it's a beautiful, colourful Mahala bead. How loving of her to do that for me. When I thanked her later, she wrote the following: "It is so wonderful to see you on Wednesday mornings! You have a beautiful energy!" Yes, yes, I do – and it does show!

Saturday

This happened on Thursday: I was eating my breakfast and heard two men yelling at each other. I went to the window to see (maybe that's the problem; maybe I shouldn't have gone to see at all) what was going on, and this young guy and old man were face to face with each other, yelling over something. They then started bumping each other, and the young guy pushed the old man down! The old man got right back up and continued his yelling. The young guy then head-butted the old man. I was so shocked, I just stared. Then a swarm of building workers approached the two men and separated them. One of the guys gave the old man a tissue, and when he pulled it away from his face, it was full of blood.

I went out and asked if they needed me to be a witness, but the workers said they'd seen it all. The workers left, and the old man asked me to watch out for the police and ambulance as he was going to his apartment for more tissue. I flagged the police down, and the old man returned with his dog, as he hadn't gone inside after all. I returned to my apartment, and ten minutes later, I heard the old man's raised voice.

Old Man: I did not touch him first! He assaulted me! What do you not understand, for God's sake?

Police #1: There's no need to raise your voice, sir.

Old Man: I'm in my seventies. I don't need this goddamned bullshit!

(I didn't hear what the police officer said after that.)

Old Man: Ok, I'm sorry, but I've told you what happened.

I had to start getting ready to go exercise. It was only 8:10 am. Sigh. I read this article yesterday, from ChurchMilitant.com:

Vatican CDF Official to Journalists: Keep Exposing Corruption

ST. PETERSBURG, Fla. (ChurchMilitant.com) - A Vatican official with a frontline view of clergy sexual abuse allegations is claiming common ground with Catholic media.

Monsignor John Kennedy, Head of the Vatican Disciplinary Section of the Congregation for the Doctrine of the Faith (CDF) since 2017, delivered the plenary address at the Catholic Media Conference in St. Petersburg, Florida Wednesday.

The Vatican official described the toll his work has had on him personally, his 17 staff members and the bishops who report cases of abuse to his office.

"I can honestly tell you that, when reading cases involving sexual abuse by clerics, you never get used to it, and you can feel your heart and soul hurting," said Kennedy. "There are times when I am pouring over cases that I want to get up and scream, that I want to pack up my things and leave the office and not come back."

"In all honesty, this work has changed me and all who work with me," he noted. "It has taken away another part of my innocence and has overshadowed me with a sense of sadness." "I have seen bishops who were once smiling pastors turned into morose, burdened figures," referring to bishops who wept when reporting cases. (Martina Moyski. 2019. "Vatican CDF Official to Journalists: Keep Exposing Corruption." Last modified June 21. https://www.churchmilitant. com/news/article/vatican-cdf-official-to-journalists-keep-exposing-corruption.)

Finally! Someone who seems to understand! Too bad the Pope doesn't come out stronger.

Of course, the journalists will continue to expose pedophiles in the church, and elsewhere. Pedophiles are a part of life, be it in the church or elsewhere.

Sunday

I went to a new class at my gym yesterday. It was a boxing class. I started talking to this man outside the class as I was new. When the class started, he and I partnered up. At one point, he told me to stop moving around. He said, "I don't like doing all that shuffling. Just stand still so I can punch properly." Oh, ok. I wasn't aware that the point of boxing was to stand still! I did not enjoy the class at all.

I was in a bad mood when I got home – had been in a bad mood all weekend. I felt hurt, angry, guilty, frustrated, and stuck. As I pulled into my parking area, there was a car parked in my spot.

No. Not today. I blocked the car and went into the building and into my apartment. I knew I'd hear whoever the idiot was when they returned as all my windows were open. Sure enough, five minutes later, a couple said, "Oh, no! We're blocked!" I was in my "Zen" room (ha ha) and opened the door onto the patio and stepped out.

Me: So that's *you* parked in my spot?

Man: Yes!

Woman: Yes!

Me: I'll be down in a minute.

I went outside, and stood in front of the car.

Me: You almost got towed.

Man: We were dropping off something for someone.

Me: That's my spot you're parked in.

Woman: We're so sorry.

Man: Normally, we park over there (pointing).

Me: That spot is actually not a parking spot.

Man: See, we thought the parking was first come, first served. We didn't know you had reserved spots.

Me (thinking, of course you didn't know, you don't live here): Yes, these are all private. You're lucky because you almost got towed.

Man: Yes. Thank you! Now we know.

It's an ongoing problem, as we have no visitor parking. But there's *lots* of parking on the street. Do not park in my spot. How's that for "beautiful energy"?

Tuesday

I'd called my friend Bev yesterday to see if she wanted to attend an event on Saturday. I was really undecided, but if she was free and wanted to go, I would. This morning I decided I didn't want to go after all. Bev called back today and asked how I was doing. I was foul, I told her. I didn't really want to go into why, but eventually, I told her I was angry that I had no idea who I was without my burden. She sympathized with me and understood how bizarre and strange it was to be free, but still be holding on tightly to the old self.

Wednesday

Wow! After the first yoga class yesterday, I decided not to stay for the second but sat down with my friend, Sue, to chat for fifteen minutes before the second class started. Sue was sitting beside a friend of hers (who'd also taken the first class). Sue asked me if I could guess the age of her friend. I thought she was probably sixty-six but didn't say anything in case she was younger. The woman smiled sheepishly and said, "I'm eighty!"

I'm sorry, *what*? She also plays some sports and showed me the huge bruise from a recent game. I felt incredibly lazy and out of shape as they both went in for the second class and I went home to rest!

Saturday

I almost got another cat today! Not on purpose, but if it was meant to be, I'd have kept the baby. It wasn't meant to be. When I went to get my coffee this morning, I saw the most beautiful dark-orange tabby. I called to the kitty, and it came close, but then ran to the next property. I figured it belonged to some idiot next door who lets his cat out.

I left, and when I returned, Betty (the gardener for our building) was doing some planting, and I offered to help. When we got to the front of the building, the kitten was back. This time, it walked over to me and allowed me to pick it up. I brought the kitten upstairs to my apartment and tried to give it some food and water, but the kitty wasn't interested. I put the kitten in a cat carrier and brought it outside. There was no collar or tags. And that's when I thought I wanted to keep baby.

Another neighbour came home and asked what was going on, and I told her. She took the kitty out and told me he was an unneutered male. No, I hadn't even bothered to check. I'd been too busy praising him for being so brave and gentle. I really don't have the money to fix him and add the extra medical expenses. So off to the Humane Society I went, hoping the kitty didn't have a chip because he shouldn't be returned to owners who are so irresponsible. (The kitty's nails were out of control too.) The poor thing was terrified but so gentle and wanting to be held.

While I was at the Humane Society, this man had to wait to see the vet about the most gorgeous dog he'd just adopted. It was an eight-month-old female Shepherd-Collie mix who was so curious about everything. She'd been given up because her previous owner found her too high energy. Um, idiot, did you not research what you were getting yourself into? The man was just over the moon in love with his new puppy. He told me he took her for four thirty-minute walks every day, and she's perfectly calm in his home. She saw my cat carrier and went up to it. I was hesitant at first, but she was silent and just sniffing it. Kitty came up to the grill and started sniffing the dog too! I told the owner, "Well, if you want a cat, you know they get along." He left, and I was seen next. They took the cat, put it in their own carrier and gave me mine back, and I left.

When I returned home, Betty was still there. She told me that an older man had asked her if she'd seen an orange kitten about. When she told him that I'd taken the kitty to the Humane Society, the older man said "Good." Apparently, it was his teenage grandson's kitten, and he said his grandson wasn't taking care of it responsibly (no kidding), so he was glad someone else would have the kitten! I'm sorry, Universe, but I hate ignorant people who discard animals.

Monday

I spent the past week meditating every day. And like I always do, once I've meditated for a while, I feel awesome. I also started doing double yoga classes again. My mind and body are starting to heal. I'm not too sure about my spirit yet, but I'm working on that!

I found a very helpful meditation about forgiveness, which is my problem area. This meditation said that if you can't forgive, have the *intention* to forgive. That I can deal with. I've been trying to forgive certain people, but it's not a true forgiveness. I'm telling myself to forgive them because I have to in order to move on. I do want to forgive them because I understand that deep (and I mean *way* down deep), they too are a divine being, but their outer masks and actions are beyond ugly. I also learned that forgiveness can take years to achieve. I had unrealistic expectations of being free and happy because I said "I forgive you" several times. Like everything else, it's a process that takes its own time.

Tuesday

What is *wrong* with people? I was in line at the drive-thru to get my coffee. I thought I heard the passenger in the car ahead of me toss out a cup of something, as I heard a thud and a splash. From my angle, I couldn't see anything on the ground, so figured I'd heard incorrectly. I got my coffee, and the car that had been ahead of me was parked to the side of the exit. As I pulled up to the car, the passenger tossed a bag of garbage onto the grass! I was beside the car and said, "Why can't you put your garbage in the bins and not on the ground?" The driver said to me, "Why don't you pick it up if it bothers you so much?" I was livid and said some not-so-nice things to the driver. So much for feeling "Zen" after my yoga class! Why must I police the world?

I reheard this acronym today: False Evidence Appearing Real. I then went online to read more about it.

From Awaken.com:

Overcoming F.E.A.R.: False Evidence Appearing Real

This self-generated fear is found in its acronym: F.E.A.R. or False Evidence Appearing Real. It appears real, even though it is a fear of the future and is not happening now. Therefore, it has no real substance, arising when the ego-self is threatened, which makes you cling to the known and familiar. Such fear creates untold worry, apprehension, nervous disorders and even paranoia.

The immediate effect of fear is to shut you down, and—in particular—to shut off the heart. (Ed and Deb Shapiro. Awaken.com. 2013. "Overcoming F.E.A.R.: False Evidence Appearing Real." Last modified January 25. https://awaken.com/2013/01/overcoming-f-e-a-r-false-evidence-appearing-real/.)

Needed this reminder today. Thanks, Universe!

Thursday

Happy Birthday, Dad. I wonder if you're proud of me. I know we're not supposed to have regrets, but I do regret not knowing my Dad. He and I always butted heads. (I think it was because we were too similar.) I feel horrible saying that he and I didn't have the kind of relationship I wished for, but that's the truth. Another problem we had was that I was too much like my Mum, and I had a tendency to nag him along with her. Poor man. Dad? Please forgive me for how I treated you. I really am sorry. I also forgive you.

Saturday

Bev and I played an escape game on Thursday, and it was so much fun! We did very well – even though we didn't solve all the rooms. What tripped us up? A very simple math equation! It was hilarious and embarrassing!

When we went for dinner afterwards, there was a family of four (Mum, Dad, and two boys, maybe five and seven) sitting in the section quite a distance across from us. The youngest did not want to eat. He started acting up and crying as his father yelled at him to eat. At one point, both boys were standing up on the booth seat marching back and forth – while both parents were on their phones. When the father realized the youngest still hadn't eaten, the whole restaurant was treated to the following:

Father (yelling): I told you to eat your chicken! If you don't eat your chicken, I'm calling security, and they're going to take you away.

Kid (starts screaming and crying): NO!

The kid hid under the table, crying his eyes out, and the father went back to looking at his phone. Eventually, the kid came out from hiding.

Father (to older child): Get your brother to eat his food!

Older Kid (arms folded over his chest, forcefully yelling): NO!

Father: I told you to get your brother to eat his food!

Older Kid: NO!

The father told the wife (who'd been on her phone) to sit with the younger one to get him to eat and went back to looking at his phone. The mother tried to get the kid to eat, but he was not having it and started screaming and crying.

Father (yelling): That's it! I've had it! I'm calling security right now, and they're taking you away!

The kid started screaming and crying again and hid under the table. The father told the mother to give both kids their tablets and then…silence.

Why did this man want kids? Did he not realize that kids require attention? And what damage has he done to his child's emotional development when his way of handling conflict is to yell and threaten his child with being taken away? And it's not a seven-year-old's responsibility to make his little brother eat!

September 2019

Monday

For a while now, I've been wanting to cleanse my apartment of all the negative and stagnant energy that I feel hanging around. I bought some sage and read up on how to cleanse properly. I love it!

Saturday

I can't believe how quickly time has gone by!

I have done so much cleansing on myself. I even had an Intuit Reiki session. After the Reiki, we sat down, and the Reiki practitioner wrote down several things she'd seen. I hadn't told her anything about myself. So, what had she seen? She asked me about the problem with my Dad (I started crying) and why I was "so pissed" at my Mother (cried again). She suggested I write letters to everyone who I was mourning.

Yesterday, I wrote everyone I needed to a letter. I also went to SAF's to tell her I could no longer see her anymore as all we did was enable each other to numb out. It sounds so stupid saying that, but it is and was the truth. I didn't want a repeat of Dolly's performance.

Saturday

I have been cleansing myself and my apartment every day and protecting myself, and it absolutely does make a positive difference. I am catching and correcting my negative thoughts. I can't even explain what a difference this has on my mood.

On Thursday, I felt really heavy with sadness – the releasing after writing the letters. I knew I wasn't finished talking to my Mum, as there was still anger. I decided to drive to the mall to find a secluded parking spot and scream and cry and write her another letter when I got home. I took a different route and came upon a church. I decided to go in – figured my Mum would get a kick out of that! I was let into the church by the side door and told there was another person inside praying. When I walked in, I quickly scanned the place but could see no one else. I sat in the very front and let the tears flow. A short while later, I heard someone walking towards the altar. She stopped, blessed herself, walked by me, saw my anguish, and said: "Oh, baby! Please don't cry. God is here for you." And I broke down and sobbed. She came over to me and put her hand on my shoulder. Then she took both her hands and held my face, saying, "It's ok, baby."

We talked for a bit, and then she started crying when telling me of her sadness. She was around seventy, and her only son had abandoned her since marrying his wife. Her son had been a true mama's boy, and his absence, cruelty, and betrayal were tearing her apart. She asked me why I didn't keep trying to mend fences with certain people, as her religious faith told her she had to keep trying with her son. I tried to explain that in order for me to be free and happy, certain people couldn't be in my life.

I came home, wrote my Mum a four-page letter and burned it. I also wrote myself a letter. I was in my Zen room when I noticed my kitty, Bowie, looking at something I couldn't see. He went onto my balcony, and a moth appeared and flew around me and landed on my shoulder. When it flew away, and I was about to step inside, I noticed two black birds fly to a nearby tree, perch on a branch, and look directly at me. I knew they were my Mum and Dad, so I told them what I needed to, and once I was finished, they flew away. Thanks, Universe!

Monday

Summer is officially over, and I'm very sad. Just the thought of having to wear socks and shoes and a jacket makes me cringe! I am now back to doing double yoga classes — today was my first one. While I wasn't sure I would be able to last through the second class, I did. Congrats to me!

I haven't released all the stress and tension of the past couple of weeks so my body still feels very stiff. With time, my body will truly let go.

I am really breaking it down as to why I should, but more importantly, need to, recognize and celebrate all my wonderfulness! Believe it or not, I was going to ask my friends why they love me so that I could understand how good I am. But it has to come *from* me. I have to learn to love me for me, and not what others see or feel about me.

It's funny because someone told me they loved me a few weeks ago, and I told them that I couldn't say it back until it was real for me. Not more than two weeks after they told me, we were talking again, and I surprised myself by telling them "I love you." It felt real and awesome. Too many times, we say "I love you too" because it's what's expected. I was telling people I loved them when they were continually hurting me, but because they told me they loved me, I would always say it back, and then wonder, "What kind of love is this that makes me feel bad about myself?"

Wednesday

Oh, my poor body! It's so sore from doing double classes these past three days. By next week, however, my body will be used to it.

I had a very interesting and significant dream last night. I was going on a trip with my Mum and her friend – though I'm not sure where we were going. We drove for a while, and then came upon a restaurant where we decided to stop and have dinner. The restaurant was a dump. We looked at the menus – and this is how cool dreams are: When you opened the menu, the actual chicken dinner with rice and veggies was on the right side and on the left side was a beef dinner with potatoes and gravy. The steam from the potatoes was rising off the menu. I decided to taste the gravy, and it was disgusting. I closed the menu and then opened it again, and the chicken and beef dinners popped up again, both steaming. My Mum and her friend decided we would eat there despite having only two choices that looked old and tired. The waitress brought us our water, and she filled the water glasses only up to one quarter and walked off. I told my Mum and her friend that that was not acceptable. She should have filled our glasses at least three quarters of the way. I went over to the waitress to complain, and then she started yelling at another waitress about our table, about how difficult we were being. I picked up my quarter-filled glass of water and went in search of the manager. I ended up having to leave the restaurant and walk all over what was now a resort with many different restaurants. After around twenty minutes, I found the main dining room and asked to speak with the manager. The girl behind the counter kept telling me there was no manager, but I refused to move until the manager spoke with me. Finally, a woman walked towards me and asked if she could help me. I told her I wanted the manager because I had a complaint to make, and she told me she was the manager.

She was grateful that I'd found her because she knew the food was horrible, but no one ever complained about it. I showed her the glass of water I'd been poured, but she didn't seem to notice it. She brought me to one restaurant but that wasn't where my Mum and her friend were.

We ended up having to go to three more restaurants before I finally found my Mum and her friend. They'd finished their dinner, and when the manager asked how it had been, they said,

"Oh, it was wonderful," and the manager left. Once the manager was out of sight, they told me that the food had been vile. I was so frustrated because it had taken me two hours to leave and come back, and my Mum and her friend hadn't been honest.

The next dream I remember (I have a feeling they were back-to-back), my Mum appeared again. We were going down an escalator, and it stopped suddenly, and my Mum was hurt. I told her I'd carry her, and I carried her up the escalator. Then, suddenly, we were in a restaurant's kitchen, and she'd turned into a baby. I kept telling her she was getting too heavy to carry, so I put her down on a counter. The chef brought me a rolling cart, and I set her down and wheeled her around, and then I woke up.

Yes, this burden I am carrying I believe is my Mum's. And it's becoming too heavy for me to carry any longer.

Thursday

Last night, a friend felt she needed to call me after I texted her goodnight. And I broke down crying. I'd told her earlier about the dreams, but as I was having my dinner, a wave of sadness overcame me and I started bawling. I even slammed some cupboard doors and punched a pillow. What set me off? I was so angry that my Mum came to me in two dreams and never once said, "I'm so sorry for what happened to you, Lee." I believe I need to hear my Mum say that. My friend told me to focus on the fact that she'd come to me in two dreams, that my Mum wanted to let me know that she's with me, and that's what I should focus on.

When I woke up this morning and stepped onto my balcony with my kitties, a butterfly appeared. It stayed on the brick as I acknowledged and thanked it for the beautiful sign. Then Kya tried to eat the butterfly, so it flew away. A friend was over for coffee, and when we were sitting on my balcony, the butterfly appeared again. My friend was amazed as it flew around my flowers and me. We watched it for a while until it settled onto the flowers next to me and stayed. We got up to go about our own day, and when I returned to the balcony, after seeing my friend out, the butterfly was still there. I closed the balcony door and ran some errands. When I got home, I immediately went to my balcony to see if the butterfly was still there, and you know what? It was! Thank you, Mum!

Friday

I had the worst dream of my life last night. It really scared me.

I dreamt that Abby (someone I once cared deeply for) and I were having a fight to the death! Seriously! One of us had to dic. It was a long and very detailed fight! Never in my life have I dreamt something that scary and real. Thankfully, I woke up before the end. Talk about up and down! Wednesday was an incredibly phenomenal day with that butterfly (my Mum), and Thursday night I'm having a nightmare.

Wednesday

I can't even explain the tension in my jaw right now!

My entire body is tense. I know it stems from a specific person I'm trying to release. The pain in my body started last week, but my jaw's been beyond tight for almost a week now. I can't seem to release the tension. I've tried meditating and even cleansing myself, to no avail.

I understand I have to be patient, Universe, but when will my body and mind finally feel relaxed and comfortable with the drastic changes I've made to my life? I've even had to stop yoga because of how stiff I feel.

Thursday

I've said it before, and I'll say it again: What a difference a day makes! When I woke up this morning, guess what? No more pain in my jaw! How's that possible? Well, I asked the Universe for help, and I knew what was causing the stress, tension, and pain.

October 2019

Friday

I had the best sleep last night and woke up super late this morning. I am finally getting the rest that my mind, body, and soul need.

It's been a bit of a rough morning though, as tomorrow will mark the anniversary of my Dad's death. Doesn't matter how many years go by, I will always miss you, Dad! Love you.

Monday

I was talking with a friend today who was extremely angry over family obligations. She was angry because of the guilt she felt for doing what was best for herself and not the family. Ah, the guilt.

Unfortunately, there's no getting around that guilt – or anger, for that matter – which is the struggle that keeps us stuck. When you decide to do what's best for yourself, do not expect others to applaud you. You're the one stepping out of the box. You're the one causing a disruption to the status quo. There's no reasoning or explaining yourself to others, especially if they're negative, controlling, and do not have your best interests at heart – which is why you're stepping out of the box in the first place. And yet, we still try to defend ourselves to these others because we want to be understood, seen, not thought of negatively, and loved.

As Christmas is fast approaching, I'm wondering how many people out there will be suffering through family gatherings with people who hurt them and make them feel less than, all for the sake of maintaining the lie that the family is still intact, important, and that ancient traditions must be adhered to. This leads to anger and then guilt regarding doing what's best for yourself. What sense does that make? Don't get me wrong, I'd love to have a family to celebrate the holidays with, but only if I genuinely felt that family loved, respected, and supported me.

What will I be doing for Xmas? Going to the movies solo and probably having spaghetti for dinner. Am I happy about that? No, actually, I'm not. It is sad. However, I love myself enough to do what's best for me. And I do love my movies and spaghetti – ask anyone who knows me.

It's not easy accepting that you'll never be understood and must go your own way. But it's wonderful knowing you'll never have to suffer through another experience of what I would characterize as a lie that causes me much lingering pain.

Wednesday

There are no coincidences, or rather, signs abound. Thank you, once again, Universe.

I decided to go online last night, and the following article was on my feed. It's a must-read and continuous reread:

From PsychologyToday.com:

You cannot love someone else until you learn to love yourself

Self-love comprises four aspects: self-awareness, self-worth, self-esteem and self-care. If one is missing, then you do not entirely have self-love. To have it, we should be aligned with these four aspects.

Self-Worth

… "There is never a day that you are not worthy. Self-worth is not determined by anything; you don't have to do anything to be worth it. You just are. Know that and understand that."

Self-Esteem

Self-esteem has everything to do with being content and comfortable with who you are, where you are, and what you have.

Ask yourself this question as often as you can: "What would someone who loves themselves do?" Ask yourself this question whenever you need to make a decision, be it trivial or important. This exercise will come with one tip and one warning.

Tip: Trust your instinct; your inner self knows best.

Warning: You will not always like what your instinct tells you to do. (Sarah-Len Mutiwasekwa. PsychologyToday.com. 2019. "You cannot love someone else until you learn to love yourself." Last modified November 12. https://www.psychologytoday.com/ca/blog/the-upside-things/201911/self-love.)

Thursday

How do I go about healing my fear? By understanding what's at its core, which I think is self-worth. I've been repeating the following mantra all day: What would someone who loves themselves do? I like this approach better than trying to think positively. It's the same difference, but for me, saying, "What would someone who *loves* themselves do?" goes deeper. I am asking my mind to imagine a loving scene, and that's the pause I hope will redirect my thoughts.

Saturday

Unbelievable, Universe! I am so friggin' hurt, angry, and shocked!

What happened? I went somewhere and was waiting for someone else, when I heard a family member's voice. I absolutely froze, and then panicked. I rose from the chair I'd been sitting on and went to the closet where I'd put my coat. I listened as this family member talked and sat down. I exited the closet, looked at who I was supposed to have been seeing, mouthed something, and left.

The encounter was purely coincidental, since I set up the appointment yesterday out of the blue.

But as we all know by now, there are no coincidences, so that encounter was destined to be.

I started crying the minute I left the area and couldn't stop. I went to the store (for what, Lee?) to get whatever. Where was my mantra, "What would someone who loves themselves do?" Nowhere. In that moment, it was fight or flight and get what you need to calm yourself down.

I started getting agitated because the queue in the store was all over the place. When a man who'd already paid stood in front of me waiting for his friend to pay, I told him, "You're in my way," with tears running down my face. Yes, indeed. He apologized. I then told someone who'd just joined the queue that I would be next after the girl he stood behind. He apologized also and stood behind me. He said to me:

Guy: Bad day?

Me (tears still flowing): Yes.

Guy: It could be worse.

Me: I could be dead?

Guy: Do you know the band Blah Blah?

Me: No.

Guy: Check out the song Blah. You should really check it out.

Me: Thanks, I will. And I'm sorry about before.

Went and got my coffee, and the regular servers saw my tears and offered me a hug, and another wrote "smile" on the lid of my cup.

When I got home, I looked up the song. It didn't help, as I wasn't in the mood for the message. However, it was very thoughtful and kind of that guy to try to make me feel better despite my rudeness. Why so rude, Lee?

I went somewhere else for the appointment I'd walked out of. The woman I saw was quite chatty:

Woman: Oh, I just love Christmas music. Some people here don't, but I do.

Me: I love Christmas music too.

Woman: Christmas is all about family. It's the best time of year for me. Do you have a big family?

Me: No. I'm alone.

Woman: What about your husband?

Me: I'm single.

Woman: But you're so pretty! Why are you not married? Do you have kids?

Me (wondering what being pretty has to do with anything): Nope, not married yet and no kids.

Woman: What about your parents, siblings?

Me: My parents have passed. It's *just* me.

Woman: Oh! You're so brave! Sometimes I wonder why I got remarried.

Brave? I get so bloody tired of people looking at me like I'm some kind of anomaly.

Sunday

It was a rough night.

I did a sage-cleanse before going to bed and listened to an amazing meditation while in bed. I still woke up and started to cry. Hearing that family member's voice really hurt, Universe.

What would someone who loves themselves do? They'd allow the hurt to rise and remind themselves they will be ok. So that's what I'm doing.

Monday

I'm doing much better today, but didn't go to yoga, even though I got up intending to. The mantra is helping and I've been meditating.

On Saturday, I truly was a zombie. I spent the day just watching TV or staring at a wall, still trying to process hearing that voice and all that it brought up.

Tuesday

I worked out today, which was a mistake. I couldn't concentrate during the first class and started crying in the second class. I am still so very hurt.

Wednesday

I am feeling much better today! I actually woke up feeling great about myself. I did another sage cleanse last night.

I thought I was enjoying the most beautiful meditation until the scene switched. I'd been guided to imagine my future self full of love and happiness. It was wonderful, and I felt myself smiling for a good five minutes. I was then guided to imagine a beautiful holiday scene. I was told to imagine my entire family (including grandparents) at this beautiful holiday scene. I stopped the meditation immediately. How about someone make a meditation that acknowledges that many people are family-less. Why shouldn't I still be able to imagine a beautiful holiday scene without family! Leave it to me to imagine who I want there. No, this hasn't dampened my mood.

Wednesday

What are you *so* scared of?

I wish I could answer that, I really do. But there's no logical or illogical explanation. I have been practicing positive self-talk, and it works – I've been feeling so much better. I've finally released the encounter. The meditations are incredibly inspiring and helpful, and yet …yet, *what*, Lee?

From PsychologyToday.com:

What Makes Your Life Meaningful and Fulfilling? What I used to get wrong when I discussed single life, including my own

The way I used to think about my life — I'm not married, but I have friends and relatives; I'm not a parent, but I have ties to the next generation — showed the opposite of what I had hoped. I was not free of the blueprint at all. I had unwittingly accepted the premise that a spouse and children should be at the center of adult life and tried to cast my own life as a reasonable approximation to that ideal.

I am also deeply fulfilled by an aspect of my life that is supposed to scare me out of being single. I am alone. I don't mean that I don't have friends or relatives who matter to me — I do. I mean that I live alone. At 65, I'm still figuring out how to break completely free of the marriage-plus-children blueprint for how to live, and how to evaluate a life. (Bella DePaulo. PsychologyToday.com. 2019. "What Makes Your Life Meaningful and Fulfilling? What I used to get wrong when I discussed single life, including my own." Last modified March 3. https://www.psychologytoday.com/ca/blog/living-single/201903/what-makes-your-life-meaningful-and-fulfilling.)

I.

Am.

Alone.

And there's absolutely nothing wrong with that. I am not an anomaly. I have chosen to create my own blueprint for my own life. Thank you, Universe.

Sunday

I'm learning to accept the grief I'm in. Having been adopted, it's really hard wrapping my head around what's happened – regardless of the necessity. The hurt of being abandoned is real for me.

Someone asked me if I could get in touch with my birth mother or natural sister. I can't, but more importantly, I don't need or want to. They're not my family either. And why would you ask me that?

As they say, "This too shall pass." But *when*, Universe? This feeling of being rejected is breaking my heart. And that's what's so hard to comprehend. I did nothing wrong! I just told the truth of what I experienced. The ties that bind are brutal! Why the hell am I crying over this? Because, Lee, you're hurting and grieving. Accept that and stop fighting it. I guess I'll be doing another sage cleansing tonight. Sigh! Accept the grief, Lee. There's nothing else you can do. And then, remember what this chapter is entitled.

November 2019

Monday

I allowed the grief to overtake me. I was in bed by 7:30 pm – couldn't even eat the dinner I'd prepared. I did two beautiful meditations and slept. I woke up this morning feeling so much lighter! That was a deep release, which was long overdue. Thank you, Universe.

Thursday

To My Molester,

You've invaded my dreams quite enough now. I wonder if I invade your dreams? I must. Do you dream about the little girl playing with your penis, etc.? Oh. You think that's a vulgar and disgusting thing to think about, let alone write? You taught me to do those vulgar and disgusting things to you.

Your arrogance and ignorance when believing I should be over it by now is that of all molesters. For molesters, it's just a momentary, gratifying sexual experience. Several years ago, I was at my breaking point and questioning if this life was for me. Your "momentary, gratifying sexual experience" almost cost me my life! I am so happy that I will never have to see you again.

Lee

I'm just so sick and tired of molesters, rapists, and sexual abusers and their lies and believing they're untouchable.

Thursday

Universe? You know what happened the other day. I really wasn't expecting to feel so sad after spending time with Bob and Alice. I'm supposed to let them go too? Will my heart never stop breaking? Help me to not dwell on them because they're not an urgent release or loss. I am so tired of saying goodbye to people, regardless of whether it's for my highest good.

December 2019

Saturday

Last night, I had that false dream again with John and Jane. Once again, I was with John somewhere, and Jane appeared out of nowhere. Next thing I knew they were looking lovingly at each other right in front of me – as if I didn't exist. Man, the jealousy and hurt I feel in the dream is so real.

I know, Universe. Like that dream, my fears are just as false and are not based on/in reality. They sure make you feel as if they are though, don't they? False Evidence Appearing Real? Indeed.

A few days ago, I came across a picture of myself that I've always loved. I'm either four or five. A "before" picture. I put it beside my laptop where I write. I've stared at that child for days now trying to reconcile something. What? I'm not sure. I've put the picture away now. Her story is finally being heard.

Monday

It's ridiculous that as Christmas approaches, I've been stressing myself. I just want the day to be over with already! Ugh. This is my first Christmas understanding that family celebrations are finished for me. I've been crying and can't focus on anything. I've tried to convince myself that it's just another day, and really, it is. But, it's not in my heart.

Friday

Christmas was horrible. Boxing Day was worse. All I did was cry and sleep.

Tuesday

Someone wanted me to explain how my book would make any money, as it's well known that authors tell woes of not making any money until their third or fourth book. I honestly had no answer. I freaked myself out regarding my finances, even though I'd already decided to go back to working part-time in April. I won't lie, I dream that this book will make money. Why shouldn't that be a dream? But then I started doubting myself and the message I'm hoping to spread, so I started looking for a job. There was not one single job that was anywhere near interesting. I decided to update my resume to include the two previous jobs I'd had.

January 2020

Friday

I am so proud of myself!

Some family members were in my dreams last night and wanted me to reconcile with them. During my dream, each one tried to guilt and harass me into being a part of their lives again. I unequivocally said no way! I told them we were done. It felt so good! Thank you, subconscious mind for being aligned with my conscious mind.

When I told a friend about the above dream, he said, "You shouldn't completely close the door. You should leave it open a bit, just in case. A loving heart blah, blah, blah." Ironically, this is the same guy who questioned my love for a family I'm not tied to by blood. Sigh. It's because I have a loving heart that I must close the door. Will no one ever understand this? No, Lee, probably not, as you're not living in the false world that insists families are perfect and loving.

Tuesday

There are *no* coincidences! You're very funny, Universe!

As I mentioned before, I've been freaking out about working and trying to quiet my mind.

I received two different voicemails today, both from unknown numbers. These two people knew me by name, but neither message made any sense to me, and I couldn't place the voices. Turns out my replacement from my last job gave notice yesterday and is moving away. Um, ok.

My old boss wanted to know if I knew anyone for the job and if I could help him out until he found someone. I told him

I didn't know anyone but would help him out until he found someone else.

Um, Lee? Didn't that job stress your mind, body, and spirit? It most certainly did. But I can do it for two weeks, three tops. Plus, my mind really needs something to keep it occupied for a bit.

And now, I have a great reference. Thanks, Universe!

Wednesday

I woke myself up twice during the early morning thinking about going back to work. I am only there temporarily. I have to keep reminding myself of that fact. I am grateful for the income and opportunity to focus on something else.

Thursday

I called my friend, Diane, to update her on my life. She was so supportive. She remarked on the wonders of life's opportunities. (Just last week we'd met, and I shared with her my financial insecurities.)

Sunday

Yesterday, I reacquainted myself with the job, plus there was a lot of work to be done. I was quite impressed with myself at how quickly I remembered everything. It did take a bit to remember all the terminology but, thankfully, my replacement kept the handbook I'd created.

Tomorrow I go into the office, and I'll admit, I'm nervous. On Thursday, I almost wanted to change my mind about helping out. You've got this, Lee. Thanks, Universe.

Tuesday

I cried when I got home from the office yesterday. Sigh. It was completely overwhelming seeing so many people yesterday, having the new computer freeze frequently and forgetting how to do things.

My jaw tightened as I sat down to work today knowing all that had accumulated. I started getting upset until I remembered the wise words from Diane: "I'm in the driver's seat." I am? Wait a minute! I'm just helping out. I have a set number of hours a week! Thanks, Universe!

Sunday

What an insane week!

Even though I am doing only my set hours, it's a lot, and the stress is incredible. I can't shut my mind off regarding all that needs to be done this week. Plus, yoga has taken a back seat, as it's easier to work in the morning to mid-afternoon. Meaning the one thing that I absolutely love and helps me relax is gone. Barbados, Lee. That's why you're doing this. Yes, I am taking myself on another beach vacation.

Monday

I'm beginning to wonder if the Caribbean is even worth going through this job again. Oh, Universe!

I am not in a good space at all. I know I need to learn how to manage stress, but there are extenuating circumstances that I could never have foreseen with just helping out. I wish I could share because it's unbelievable and overwhelming and I'm in a rage. And this is supposed to be an opportunity?

I will say this though: journaling about your intimate views and faults and where you are at this stage of your life is great!

Note this book. However, journaling about your intimate views and faults and where you are at this stage of your life should never be left on the company's computer. Someone else with the work computer could be looking for a work-related document and come across this extremely personal and private journal. Indeed.

Wednesday

I tried to remain upbeat as I started working today. It didn't last very long. I know hating it is the wrong approach, so instead, I'll just start the countdown: five more business days until I train the new girl, and one more office day for life. Let me be very clear that it's not my boss – he's fantastic – it's the workload.

On a happier note, I broke out laughing when listening to the voicemail of a client: "You have reached the number you dialed." Too true! Misdialed or not! Ha!

Friday

Sigh, sigh, sigh.

I've had to take an Advil every day – sometimes twice – as my jaw is in a vice grip. Three more working days, two training days, and one more office day. My weekend has officially started, and I've put the work computer in the closet – don't even want to see it! And I've turned off my phone (maybe for the entire weekend). I am in my pajamas and on the couch or napping for the next two glorious days.

Wednesday

Two training days left and one more office day. Amen.

February 2020

Friday

Relief!

Training is done. The replacement got the job quickly, having had previous experience with this specific position. I am going to have to do some serious releasing from this experience. I have such deep emotions regarding the extenuating circumstances. I think that's what I'll do this weekend – write privately about it, burn the damn thing and then do a cleanse. One more office day.

Sunday

Why, Universe? I am *angry*! Went to remote-start my car and … *nothing*!

Once again, it's too cold for the damn stupid car! A kind stranger helped me jump-start it, but the engine and service light are now on with "transmission malfunction." I don't dare drive it to the office tomorrow and will have to take Uber. I'll then have to bring it to the shop on Tuesday, just like what happened last year. Nice.

Monday

Today was my last day at work. It's over. Enough said.

Wednesday

I'm feeling very sad. Why? Valentine's Day and people in general. Why, Universe? Why have I never had anyone in my life I could truly rely on to always be there for me, no matter what or when. This fact makes me so sad.

Friday

I received an incredible reference letter from my boss. I was actually extremely proud that my professionalism and character were so wonderfully reviewed.

I've done a lot of reflecting today, the day of love.

My dream of going to the Caribbean was almost lost due to the expense. I found another island that looked beautiful and cost $2500.00 less. Indeed. I'd planned on booking it tomorrow, when I realized I didn't want to go anywhere other than where I dreamt of going. So, I'm going to my dream island! Yeah!

7:30pm

Once again, there are no coincidences! You're funny, Universe! I got a text from another "friend," someone I was supposed to have released ages ago, someone to whom I'm an afterthought. The text said, "I know it's last minute but…" But what? If you want to see me, let's plan to get together. I am a forethought, not an afterthought.

Letting go of emotional connections is going to take me time to overcome. No kidding, Sherlock! Today, I accepted having to release two more "friends"! Will it never end? Not as long as any relationship confuses or hurts you, Lee. I was angry, upset, and cried over the losses. Time will heal my wounds. Since I started this third book, I've released more than eighteen people. My phone book's almost empty!

Saturday

Oh, Universe! I don't know what to say! Thank you, obviously!

When I got home, my neighbour pulled in at the same time. I smiled and said hello, expecting that to be the end of it. Not quite! He said, "I'm glad I ran into you. I wanted to wish you a Happy Valentine's Day. Please give this to your husband and kids." He told me that I'm so sweet. I'm always smiling with a pleasant greeting. Ok, I should have lied and just said thank you, but I didn't. And then we had to go through the "Why aren't you married? Why are you single?" Ugh! Anyway, he gave me a cake! Not just any cake either! It's my absolute favourite birthday cake: Black Forest! I must agree with you, Universe, feeling happy is so much better than feeling sad! Thanks again, Universe, for the kindness of strangers.

Monday

Ouch, Universe!

In the past three days, two people told me not to hold onto judgements. Recognizing that I have been judging everyone I released is quite humbling. Actually, not just judging those I've released, but judging everyone, all the time. I will be doing an ego-judging cleanse tonight. Growing up is so hard!

We can't seem to understand our emotions without feeling we've been attacked and must attack back. It's almost impossible to remember that other people are going through their own problems and need space from you too. It's hard not to take it personally, and so the mind creates crazy scenarios as to what will happen the next time you speak (or don't speak). So much wasted time and energy. And if you believe it *is* personal? Staying in judgement, anger, and sadness is absolutely about you, and not them. It's, always, only about you.

Friday

Oh, Universe! Again, I don't know what to say!

I started writing this third book because I'd cracked from my second-to-last job, which I found too stressful. I wrote that the people were awesome, and they still are! I'd asked the manager there if he'd be willing to write me a letter of recommendation and he did, gladly. I was almost in tears by his beyond-glowing and heartfelt words of my character, abilities, and contribution. Wow!

I am really starting to see – but more importantly, believe in – how wonderful a being I am. Every now and again, I'll just smile and say, "I'm so proud of myself." I have irrefutable truth that the negative critic in my head constantly lies to me. Thank you so much, Universe!

Sunday

I must say, I am thoroughly enjoying these feelings of happiness. It's also refreshing to understand that I'm not just good enough, I'm actually bloody brilliant!

Monday

Ouch! I totally wiped out on the ice yesterday! I got out of my car and started walking, and my left leg slipped out from under me. Down I went, hard, on my left hip. I had my coffee in my right hand and managed not to spill a drop!

During yoga this morning, my left wrist and left hip were too sore to do two classes. I am beyond ready for winter to be done with!

I can't believe that in three weeks from today, I'll be on my way to the Caribbean! I won't exercise tomorrow, but instead will take myself to a movie.

Thursday

I'd like to stop analyzing everything.

Within the last two days, I've told several people different funny stories that pertained to what we were talking about. Each of the stories involved two of my siblings. I had no idea that the stories would pop out of me. As I told the story and said the word sibling, there was a pause inside me (not noticeable to whom I was speaking). I was shocked I'd brought them up.

Not everything always has to mean something. The stories really were funny. End of story, Lee. And since they happened two days ago, why are you still thinking about it, Lee?

March 2020

Tuesday

I've been feeling lost for some reason. I can't even focus my mind. Yesterday, I couldn't find my headband and scrunchie for yoga that I always keep in my yoga bag. I have more, so it wasn't an issue. Later, I went to get a cat toy out of the cat box, and there my headband and scrunchie were. Um…ok. I'd left my water bottle at the gym. Sigh. Went back to the gym, and I couldn't find it anywhere. The guy at the front desk said he looked in the lost and found, but it wasn't there. But did he really look properly? I searched all the places I'd been at the club, but barring having left it in class (there was a class in session), it wasn't anywhere. I searched my car, and I searched my place, but it's nowhere. Unfortunately, the same guy was on duty when I went for yoga today. He assured me that my water bottle still hadn't been found. I asked to see the lost and found, but that's against their policy. Of course it is. Who'd want to steal someone else's water bottle? I mean, seriously.

When I got home from class, I searched my place again, but to no avail. The water bottle has vanished. I went to the grocery store to buy some things and was talking with the regular teller and went to leave – without paying. Focus, Lee.

I've decided not to try to look for a job in the Caribbean (that'd been my plan) – not with this coronavirus going on. What a nightmare. I'm a slight germaphobe.

Wednesday

Un-bloody-believable! Yesterday, I forgot my running shoes at the gym! Sigh. But thankfully, when I went back today, they'd been turned in! Whew! Still no water bottle though. It's gone, Lee. Stop looking for it. That sounds like a metaphor to me. What's causing me to be so absentminded?

Friday

What is going on with this coronavirus?

I went to the grocery store this morning to pick up one thing, and the parking lot was almost full. I wondered if it was a holiday. Inside the store, I watched masked and gloved people buying with a sense of panic. When I commented to a clerk near me that I'd never seen the store so busy this early, she replied, "It started last night. We've made more money in the last twenty-four hours than we did for the entire Christmas week. We have one distributor for 1000 stores, and the shelves are becoming bare." When I told her I'd only come in for one thing, she suggested I get a cart and load up because who knew when the shelves would be restocked. I personally can't remember a time when I've witnessed world panic at this level. If permitted, I still plan on going to the Caribbean.

Sunday

Sigh. It is not permitted. The Caribbean has to be postponed.

Healing is very interesting, as it cannot be rushed. We accept this for physical healing, but not emotional healing. I've been so unfocused recently because the timetable I allotted myself to get over the past isn't in sync with the Universe's. And that's completely changing this story.

Perhaps, that's the point. According to Julia-Chritina's Uță, in a June 27, 2019 Brand Minds article, the self-improvement industry is estimated to grow to $13.2 billion by 2022.

Real and lasting growth (change) first requires an understanding of yourself. You can't change what you won't acknowledge. This story needed to be rewritten three times over many years, and it's constantly changing as I learn more about myself.

Last year, I'd told myself I would be living my new life, in a new area, by the summer. I'm not moving anywhere for a while. I no longer need to. I am exactly where I need to be in order to heal. All my dreams will be manifested in divine and appropriate timing, not because I've created a deadline. I am being forced to slow down. The coronavirus has forced the world to slow down.

Monday

I went to yoga this morning, and the club is "closed until further notice." I understand completely.

I wanted to share the following story from the NYTimes.com:

He Has 17,700 Bottles of Hand Sanitizer and Nowhere to Sell Them

On March 1, the day after the first coronavirus death in the United States was announced, brothers Matt and Noah Colvin set out in a silver S.U.V. to pick up some hand sanitizer. Driving around Chattanooga, Tenn., they hit a Dollar Tree, then a Walmart, a Staples and a Home Depot. At each store, they cleaned out the shelves.

Mr. Colvin said he had posted 300 bottles of hand sanitizer and immediately sold them all for between $8 and $70 each, multiples higher than what he had bought them for. To him, "it was crazy money." To many others, it was profiteering from a pandemic.

Now both the physical and digital shelves are nearly empty.

"Price gouging is a clear violation of our policies, unethical, and in some areas, illegal," Amazon said in a statement. "In addition to terminating these third-party accounts, we welcome the opportunity to work directly with states attorneys general to prosecute bad actors."

Mr. Colvin does not believe he was price gouging. While he charged $20 on Amazon for two bottles of Purell that retail for $1 each, he said people forget that his price includes his labor, Amazon's fees and about $10 in shipping. (Alcohol-based sanitizer is pricey to ship because officials consider it a hazardous material.)

He added, "Just because it cost me $2 in the store doesn't mean it's not going to cost me $16 to get it to your door."

But what about the morality of hoarding products that can prevent the spread of the virus, just to turn a profit?

Mr. Colvin said he was simply fixing "inefficiencies in the marketplace." Some areas of the country need these products more than others, and he's helping send the supply toward the demand. (Jack Nicas. NYTimes.com. 2020. "He Has 17,700 Bottles of Hand Sanitizer and Nowhere to Sell Them." Last modified March 14. https://www.nytimes.com/2020/03/14/technology/coronavirus-purell-wipes-amazon-sellers.html.)

It turns out that public outcry and maybe legal ramifications forced Mr. Colvin to donate his stash. If price gouging really is forbidden, then how did Mr. Eric, a truck driver from Ohio, end up making $40,000.00 in weeks selling twenty-dollar ten-pack tissues for $125.00? To me, a 525% increase amounts to an "unconscionably excessive price." Wikipedia, the free encyclopedia, defines unconscionability as "a doctrine in contract law that describes terms that are so extremely unjust, or overwhelmingly one-sided in favor of the party who has the superior bargaining power, that they are contrary to good conscience."

The greed of people is disgusting. And, of course, the coronavirus scams have begun. Humans can't seem to grasp the concept of a conscience. The coronavirus should teach people that we are all connected. When the next pandemic occurs, will history repeat itself? Technically, the next pandemic could be avoided, but that would require honesty and world cooperation. I do like to dream.

Tuesday

I'm so disgusted!

Met a new male friend. In no way was I interested in him romantically whatsoever. I thought I was extremely clear on that.

Today, we got together at a cafe to play backgammon. We were sitting at the table, and he offered to get me some water. When he walked by me with the water, he touched my neck, and I jumped. He thought it was funny. When he got up again for something else and returned to the table, he touched my neck again, and again I jumped. This time I told him, "Don't touch me!" He said, "Don't touch you? I'm just playing around." I replied that I didn't like his playing around. He suggested we play one more game, but I was feeling too uncomfortable, so I said I had to leave (after winning, of course). As I stood up and gathered my game and purse, he stood up too.

Him: I should smack your ass for that beatdown.

Me: I really did annihilate you!

And…he smacks my ass!

Me: Don't do that.

And he goes to do it again, and I move out of the way.

Me: I said, don't do that.

Him (looking perplexed): Hey! I'm just being playful! It's just as friends!

Me: Ya, that's not cool.

He apologized profusely, and I could tell he was sorry. Except, he truly did not understand why I would take offense to him touching me playfully, "just as friends."

I truly do not understand why he thought he had any right to touch me.

Wednesday

It really isn't, but it sure does feel like it's the end of days. I went to get my kitties' food. I called ahead because of the new restrictions. I paid over the phone, was told to call once I arrived in the parking lot, and they'd bring the food to me. And that's exactly what happened. I was super lucky I called today, as I purchased the last bag until their next shipment. Panic on cat food too, naturally. When I stepped out of the car to take the bag from the man, he couldn't back away from me fast enough, so I got back in my car. Sigh. I had to prepurchase my next bag while there because of the panic.

I was glad to hear that a reporter finally asked the question that had been bothering me once the coronavirus went viral:

When will the Chinese government be held accountable for the spread of coronavirus?

On Sunday night, the two remaining Democratic Presidential candidates, Joe Biden and Bernie Sanders, entered a sparse CNN studio for a one-on-one debate, in which the venue, context, and substances were all unsurprisingly hijacked by the coronavirus pandemic. Among the top issues were how millions of Americans would endure economic stresses caused by the outbreak and what the United States government should do to overcome it, especially with the projected costs running into the trillions of dollars.

One of the debate's most interesting moments came when CNN reporter Dana Bash asked the two candidates: "What consequences should China face for its role in this global crisis?" (Marcus Kolga. macleans. ca. 2020. "When will the Chinese government be held accountable for the spread of coronavirus?" Last modified March 17, 2020. https://www.macleans. ca/opinion/when-will-china-be-held-accountable-for-coronavirus/.)

They should be held responsible. There will be another pandemic, of that you can be sure. I'm not including the article here, but by now you've all heard that China has endorsed a conspiracy theory blaming 300 US Military athletes for bringing the disease with them when they attended the 7th Military World Games in Wuhan.

Excuse me, President Trump, but referring to the virus as "the Chinese Virus" is consciously *racist*, as many have publicly stated. Ok, so honesty and cooperation are off the table.

Dispense with the blame games and work together to contain it from the second you know there's something not right, which, for the coronavirus was first identified in Wuhan, Hubei, China, in December 2019. In 2019.

You have to value lives over lies. I think it's time the world grew up. I'm not talking about this anymore. There's no point. I've lost those happy feelings I was learning to experience. It's time to get them back!

Friday

Ok, two more rants regarding the coronavirus:

Currency: By now it's apparent that money means nothing. So why not just have one economy for the world. We all need food, housing, healthcare, and education. Why is there a class system?

Entertainment vs Life: I love going to a movie. That's my thing. I also love watching certain sporting events. We all love some form of entertainment that brings us joy. But when entertainment trumps education, I have a problem and believe it's time we devalued entertainment salaries to revalue education and healthcare salaries.

I found this from Collegegrad.com:

Epidemiologists: Career, Salary and Education Information, 2020

Epidemiologist: Epidemiologists are public health professionals who investigate patterns and causes of disease and injury in humans. They seek to reduce the risk and occurrence of negative health outcomes through research, community education and health policy.

<u>Salary</u>: The median annual wage for epidemiologists is $70,990. (Collegegrad.com. 2021. "Epidemiologists: Career, Salary and Education Information, 2020." https://collegegrad.com/careers/epidemiologists.)

How much does a teacher make? In my opinion, without teachers there's no world progress. The answer? Anywhere from $30,000 to less than $61,000 annually. How much do taxi drivers make? Around $61,000 annually. An Uber driver can make up to $90,000 in certain locations. Who is the highest-paid NBA basketball player? From BusinessInsider.com:

The 24 highest-paid players in the NBA for the 2018–19 season

For the second-straight season, Stephen Curry is the NBA's highest-paid player. **Team**: Golden State

Warriors. **Position**: Point Guard **Contract**: 5 years, $201.2 million

One thing to know: Curry's $201 million contract was the largest in NBA history at the time of its signing, a huge pay bump from what was the biggest bargain in the NBA. (Cork Gaines. BusinessInsider.com. 2018. "The 24 highest-paid players in the NBA for the 2018–19 season." Last modified November 30. https://www.businessinsider.com/nba-highest-paid-players-2018-10.)

No disrespect to Mr. Curry, but the incredible skills he possesses playing a game – a game on hold indefinitely – aren't where $201.2 million over five years should be spent. It just doesn't seem right to me. We are being given an opportunity to really rethink what's most important. And the answer should be: Life. Nature can't be controlled by governments. And when nature speaks, we all have to listen. And education for *all* is key! A market should never have dead and live animals for sale side-by-side. Shouldn't that just be known? How would you know if you've not been educated and know only one way of living?

Saturday

We're living in different times, so compensation for the elderly has been made for them to be able to shop before everyone else. That makes sense.

Here's what doesn't make sense to me: having the liquor stores open earlier than normal too. And liquor stores are considered essential. Why? I've been told it's because of the detox from alcohol, which can cause death.

I believe addictions are the result of some form of trauma. But people say addictions are the result of mental health issues. Regardless, we accept and understand the term physical health. Why can't people accept and understand the term mental health? We need the type of funds given to basketball players put into mental wellness just as much as education.

April 2020

Tuesday

I'm not doing that great. I have been freaking myself out because of the coronavirus. The fear is intense. So much so that I've started having wicked panic attacks.

I've forced myself to stop checking my account as it's lost thousands due to the market. (I bet you wish you hadn't wasted all those thousands now, eh Lee?)

There are so many rapid layoffs as well as businesses having to close for good – as in, we can't recover no matter what or when the coronavirus ends.

Trust me, I am extremely grateful for all that I do have, as others are having an even harder time with their finances and lives. But I'm just afraid, you know? Anxiety breeds more anxiety. I can't control what's happening – I can control only my response. And I've been giving in to the world's panic of this life-altering pandemic.

Monday

I went on Facebook and looked up some family members. Lee? Why would you *do* that? Why am I human, you may as well ask? I wasn't on for long, as I knew it wasn't a healthy choice. It hurt, but not as much as in the past.

I had wanted to finish this book months ago so that I could move on. I can move on, but there continues to be more healing and releasing to do. It's taken almost half a dozen years and three books to work through my past and learn to rebuild myself. Would you buy a self-help book that tells you the process could take years and years? That's why it's a billion-dollar-a-year industry. I continue to move forward and can appreciate and feel the difference of my progress.

Wednesday

I had the most incredible experience of my life! What am I referring to?

Pure Silence!

I have been doing so many meditations and listening to talks about the present moment, etc. I was washing my dishes and quite suddenly, there was no stream of thought and just silence, and I was aware of the silence. My mind said, "Oh my God," and I said to myself, "Stop!" and refocused on the silence. It was beautiful! It may not have lasted long, but it was my first experience of pure silence. Thanks once again, Universe!

Monday

Today I cried a lot. It had been building. That's the thing about surrendering. There's no build-up if you surrender. But I resisted, so it persisted. I've been in a funk now for quite a while.

I can't remember the last time I felt any happiness, let alone joy.

Thursday

I've had a rough morning.

In the span of fifteen minutes, I had three separate opportunities to practice detachment, but chose to react instead. Driving home (from where, Lee?) somebody almost cut me off. I did a blasting honk and immediately switched lanes. As the person pulled up beside me, he rolled down his passenger window, and I gave him the finger and drove ahead of him to the stoplight. He was behind a car and I wasn't, so that ended that confrontation. Good for you, Lee. You won. Right?

I was almost home when I saw the ass-slapping guy. (I'd told him I would not be in his presence again after that incident.) We saw each other, and I averted my eyes and thought, "What an absolute loser!" and other mean thoughts until I arrived at my building two minutes later.

I turned the corner onto my street and saw a neighbour with whom I had a falling out. I waited in my car to give the person enough time to get into their apartment so we'd not have to talk. I miscalculated, and we ran into each other in the entrance. I was polite and friendly, but the person could barely manage a hello to me. I then spent time going over our history. That moment you're given to decide how to react doesn't seem to be enough time. The GreaterGood.Berkeley.edu article "What is Mindfulness?" defines mindfulness: "Mindfulness means maintaining a moment-by-moment awareness of our thoughts, feelings, bodily sensations, and surrounding environment, through a gentle, nurturing lens."

It's incredible to me all that you have to learn and practice in order to love yourself. But, I'm worth it. I'll be given more opportunities on how to react, of that I am sure. Eventually, I'll get it.

Sunday

I've been thinking about my aggression and how I have to learn to love and forgive that part of myself.

I noticed this morning that I do things aggressively: flossing my teeth or blow-drying my hair. I was blow-drying my hair and I could feel how tense I was, pulling my hair. I told myself to drop my shoulders and take my time. What's the rush? I slowed down completely and experienced the heat, comb, motion, and what my hair felt like. It may not seem like such a big deal to you, but it actually is a huge accomplishment. I was mindful of what I was doing.

All the tension I still have in my body is the fear that I'm not safe. Lee, you are safe, you can relax now. The more I remind myself of this, the less tense I feel. The less tense I feel, the lighter my heart becomes. The lighter my heart becomes, the closer I am to becoming who I truly am.

Monday

Happy Birthday, Mum.

I've been crying most of the day. I've got some very strong and mixed emotions regarding my Mum. I suppose it's natural. How could she not have protected me? How could I have been so afraid to talk to her, someone who loved me? Why was it my burden to protect her from the reality that I was molested? It breaks my heart wondering why. A while ago, I threw out all my family photo albums. I only kept some photos of my parents. Thank you, Universe.

Wednesday

I was looking through Netflix and found *Cracked Up: The Darrell Hammond Story*. Obviously, our experiences are completely different as well as their severity, but he explained his feelings and emotions, as if they were my own:

> No one in my family ever talked about what happened. Where I come from, the arch-enemy, the fiend, is the truth….The whole idea that someone does this terrible thing to you, and expects you not to tell, they just expect it, is astonishing. And I've said, and will always say, the worst crime is being expected not to tell. (Netflix, 2018)

They filmed Darrell doing yoga, as doing this activity has enabled him to sleep five out of seven nights:

Interviewer: What keeps you up?

Darrell: I don't know… hypervigilance? It could happen again.

Darrell (giving a speech): To wake up one morning and not be scared? Wow…fifty years scared. Fifty years! And not now! (Netflix, 2018)

Sometimes, the timing of the information is key. I've been working on releasing just what Darrell Hammond said above.

I've been dealing with this "hypervigilance" for more than four decades. I, too, *will* wake up one day "and not be scared." Thanks, Universe. It wasn't a coincidence that I found and saw that today.

Thursday

I rewatched a part of *Cracked Up: The Darrell Hammond Story* this morning because I'd been thinking of what Bessel Van Der

Kolk, MD, author of *The Body Keeps the Score* said: "If you cannot tell the truth, you have to lock that reality away. And if reality starts festering inside, it becomes, as Freud already said, a splinter in your mind. A splinter in your brain and a splinter in your soul that starts festering. And so, anything that cannot be spoken becomes an internal danger to your self…There is not one answer. Everybody needs to discover what the answer is for them, what the right message is for them. Doing things like yoga and mindfulness meditation can actually rewire the brain. Engaging your whole body is an absolutely necessary part of healing…."

I'd never heard "anything that cannot be spoken becomes an internal danger to your self" before.

May 2020

Friday

It's no joke what Darrell Hammond shared about feeling scared for fifty years.

I will no longer label myself with having a mental illness. There was never anything wrong with me. I was molested, and my experience was having been made to deny the truth I lived. It's been wonderful knowing I'm not a freak for my confused emotions and understanding of why I've always felt such fear. To see an adult still cry over his story is honest.

Saturday

It was a bit of a rough few days there.

I was sitting on my balcony with my kitties and enjoying the fresh air. I don't know what's going on with our roof, but there've been tons of birds and pigeons flying onto it. They fly so close to me that I've ducked twice and had a bird's-eye view of their underbelly – both an awesome experience.

I just looked online for what pigeons symbolize and found "Pigeon-dove-spirit-animal symbolism-and-meaning" from Dreamingandsleeping.com: "As a totem animal or spiritual animal, pigeon represents love. Dove has been a symbol of love and peace for years back and this symbolism remained even to this day. People with this totem are loving and kind with a good understanding of life and problems that others might be having. Pigeons also represent sacrifice."

Thanks, Universe, for the signs you always provide me with. The signs you need are always available to you. You just need to see and recognize them for yourself.

A while back, I created a Grateful Message Box. I painted it and everything. I wrote a list of things I am grateful for and randomly choose one each day. Today's message: *I am grateful for still believing in myself.* And the Universe, of course.

Tuesday

I've really been ruminating on certain experiences that Darrell Hammond shared about the love and fear he felt towards his parents:

"Saturday Night Live" vet Darrell Hammond shares shocking tales in new book

He honed his impressions and turned to comedy, landing on "SNL" for more than a decade despite work-inhibiting battles with drugs and alcohol. After several years of therapy, his doctors encouraged him to confront his parents about his childhood.

"When I finally summoned up the nerve to dial the number that had been etched in my memory since I was old enough to count to ten, my mother's response was simple and heartfelt: 'Don't ever call us again.'" When Hammond saw her next, she was on her deathbed. His father died soon after. (Sheila Markikar. abcnews.go.com. 2011. "Darrell Hammond Opens Up About Childhood Abuse." Last modified November 22. https://abcnews.go.com/Entertainment/darrell-hammond-opens-childhood-abuse/story?id=15008471)

It wasn't until six years after both his parents' deaths that Darrell felt safe enough to speak up and out. Victims of abuse are often discredited because of not coming forward sooner, as was my case. The (il)logic used was that if I really had been abused, I would have said something before my fifties. With loving kindness, I release the regret and mystery of why I never spoke up or out until both my parents had long passed.

Saturday

Sigh.

I understand I've recently learned a lot, which takes time to process. I've been holding my patience stone without focusing on the energy from it. Every morning I wake up, I start to cry and refuse to sit with it. I really just don't want to do this anymore.

Q: Have you learned how to Love yourself? A: No, but I am learning.

Q: Have you learned how to Believe in yourself? A: Yes and no.

Q: Have you learned how to have Faith in yourself? A: No.

Q: Have you learned how to Trust yourself? A: No.

Lee? More loving kindness is needed for yourself.

Wednesday

It's so funny how I still think I can control or dictate how my healing will occur. I did cry yesterday and not push the emotions away, but after a while, I was bored. Patience, my child.

I asked myself a few days ago what my process was for learning something. I'd gone online to look for ways to release trauma from the body. I could do this, or I could do that. But what's best for how I learn?

I read the material while also taking copious notes. (Sometimes I feel like I'm just rewriting the book, but this way works for me, whereas flashcards don't.) I study my notes until I have an understanding. I apply what I've just learned.

As I was doing my dishes today, something about the abuse popped into my head, and I froze. My body tensed. I wanted to immediately think of something else, but I stayed with how I was feeling scared. I told myself to take some deep breaths. I told myself that in this moment, I was safe. I told myself to drop and relax my shoulders and take more deep breaths. I reminded myself over and over that I was safe. I really did feel a release.

I went out and bought flowers and have my balcony all set up. It looks fantastic – so beautiful. I bought a bicycle as cycling was a past love of mine. The weather's perfect now, so I can't wait to go bike riding.

Saturday

Let me preface this by making clear that the following are only *my* opinions. I think it's about time we made some drastic changes in the world. We've seen how the planet can very quickly recuperate when humans are forced into a timeout. I'm suggesting a new worldwide law be created to force a timeout on any more pregnancies for two years (three would be better).

According to the UN, about 385,000 babies are born each day. That means 140 million extra babies every year join a world population projected to be 10 billion people by 2056. (I got this information from the article "How Many Babies Are Born a Day?" on a website called The World Counts.) Everyone should go onto that site because it's staggering to watch the birth numbers increase every second.

Just think about what an incredible difference not having 130 million more people would make on the planet. *That's not fair, Lee! We want to have a baby, and that's our right!* We are learning our rights won't stop mother nature. It's time to depopulate.

Wednesday

Oh, Universe.

Mr. George Floyd was murdered.

This hatred regarding skin colour will never end. I think you really got it wrong with that one, Universe. For your next evolution, make everyone beige.

Thursday

I've been riding my bike for two days now, and I absolutely *love* it! Why didn't I do this years ago? Still no yoga. Whatever.

Today, I started out on my bike ride but couldn't move the bike! I fiddled around with the brakes (thinking they were set up too tight) and finally managed to start riding, but it wasn't an easy ride. I rode farther than the day before (yeah), but when I turned around, I could barely pedal. I got off again and did more fiddling, but the tires barely moved, so I pushed the damn thing off the path and onto a dead-end street. Great, I'd gone way farther than I'd wanted to!

Sigh. I was so mad! What did I expect for buying such a cheap-a** bike? After one block, I was having mega-problems pushing the bike, so I stopped and just stared at the damn thing thinking, "How the hell am I going to get home? There's no way I can carry that!" I was still staring at the bike when I saw a woman walk around the corner. I told her my bike wouldn't move. She looked at the bike and told me she'd had the exact same model and might be able to help. And boy, did she ever! She fixed it! The problem was some silver-thingy-cap had slipped down the cable. I have to kind of manhandle my bike into my storage locker. The front has to be turned a certain way to fit, so I can see how the silver-thingy-cap slipped! She did think the brakes should be loosened. I can't believe the timing! I zoomed home! I went for a very smooth and even longer ride today! Thanks, Universe!

Sunday

I went to the curbside pickup at the pet store this morning for my order of cat food. I blindly pressed what I thought was the trunk button on my remote (twice by mistake), but I was wrong. I got it after the second attempt. I left the car running and got out of the car. I decided to put the food in the back seat instead of the trunk. When I went to open the back seat door, it wouldn't open. Neither would the passenger front door. I quickly went to the driver's door and, voila, locked! That first blind press had locked all the doors! I'd been on the phone with the sales lady getting my pickup ready, and she said she'd look to see if they had a coat hanger. For some amazingly unknown reason, I'd left the front passenger window open a bit. I thought I'd closed all the windows when I went through some dusty construction. I'd tried to put my arm down the window, but it couldn't reach the door latch. I pulled down on the window (great, I'm going to break my window because of my scattered brain) but I didn't feel it budge. I tried one last time to squeeze my arm down the window, and this time, I got it! It hurt like hell, but who cares!

Disaster avoided! Pay attention, Lee. Thanks, Universe.

June 2020

Friday

I had my first social outing today! I got together with a good friend at her home. After a couple of hours, I knew it was time to leave, but I didn't want to. I even said, "Well, I guess it's time for me to go," to which my friend replied, "You don't want to, do you?" She's the first friend I've seen since the isolation, and it was amazing! As I drove home, I cried. I know I've got to learn and understand that "I am enough," with loving kindness, of course. But man, Universe, I feel very lonely, and I could really use a hug.

Wednesday

Last week, I must have had three different days of gut-wrenching sobs. I felt much better after each release. More than a dozen years ago, my Mum died. I knew my life would be forever changed, but there was no way I could have predicted what would follow. I miss and love you, Mum. I'm not feeling as conflicted regarding my emotions. So, things are slowly moving out and along. I didn't spend the day crying or being down. I am so proud of my progress. My grateful message for today: *I am grateful for my efforts to learn and love myself.* Thanks, Universe.

Thursday

I'm not ready, but it's now time I faced myself. Just yesterday, I almost yelled at a kid.

I was sitting on my balcony reading, when I heard a kid start yelling for his buddy:

Kid (yelling): JOHN? (No reply)

Kid (yelling): JOHN? (No reply)

Kid (yelling): JOHN? (No reply)

Kid (yelling): JOHN? (No reply)

I am not lying, but this went on for about twenty minutes as the kid sat on his stoop, then made the circuit of the complex, sat on this stoop again, and again made the circuit of the complex. I just barely restrained myself from yelling, "KID! John is obviously not around, so could you SHUT IT?" The kid was about ten years old.

Time to surrender and let go of my anger and control issues. It's not that I've been in denial of these issues, I just hoped they'd disappear without having to go *that* deep into them, because my anger runs very deep, and my temper is quick.

Friday

Saw this on my Facebook page.

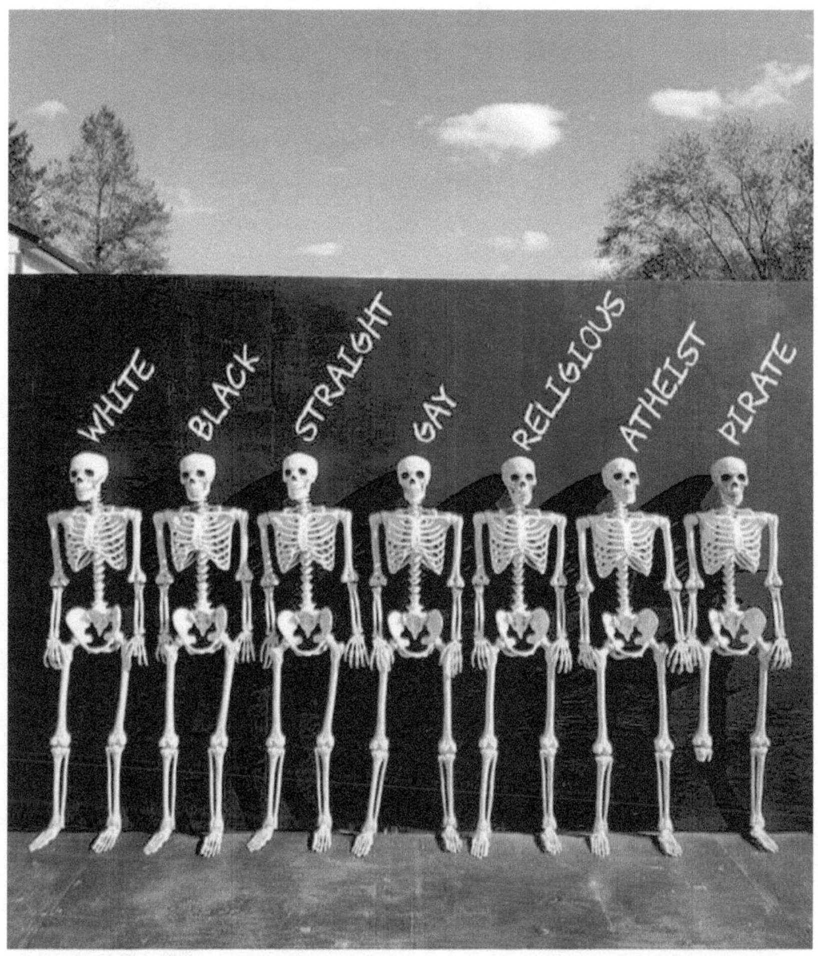

Do you know the significance of today's date? I didn't. From Wikipedia, the free encyclopedia, "What is Juneteenth?": "Juneteenth is a holiday celebrating the emancipation of those who had been enslaved in the United States. Originating in Galveston, Texas, it is now celebrated annually on the 19th of June throughout the United States, with varying official recognition. It is commemorated on the anniversary date of the June 19, 1865 announcement by Union Army general Gordon Granger, proclaiming freedom from slavery in Texas."

Again, Universe, next go around, beige. I mean, it's 155 years on. Aren't even *you* getting tired and bored with this never-ending colour hate?

Here's my suggestion: In my opinion, the United(?) States should combine nineteen (guesstimate) states. These combined states are for whites only, and their old world will be called Hostile Attitudes Towards Everyone (**HATE**). The remaining states will form the new world called People Everywhere Are Celebrated Equally (**PEACE**). Put up a border and be done with it once and for all.

Sunday

Happy Father's Day, Dad.

This day no longer represents a family day to try to get through without memories of the past flooding in. It's truly your day, Dad. I want to thank you for being my Dad. I am very proud to be your daughter.

Sunday

I'm so bloody furious!

Yesterday, I ran into Jake at the corner store. (Jake is someone I met last year and we went on one date. I thought he was an extremely attractive black man, but he was always too busy [in a relationship?] so I stopped speaking with him.) We said hello to each other and chatted through my purchase, then his purchase, and out of the store. He told me he wasn't as busy now (relationship over?) so we exchanged numbers for the second time.

We talked today. I'd forgotten how he would always bring the conversation back to one particular subject he felt he was an expert on. I was so bored listening to him that I interjected with, "Right, that's why we need to do fun things. Do you have a garden? I've got a beautiful garden on my balcony, and I love sitting outside in the sun…" and I was cut off:

Jake: You sound like a white woman.

Me: What?

Jake: You sound like a white woman.

Me: Why?

Jake: Black women don't sun themselves. You always see white women doing that.

I wanted to scream at him, "I'm a bloody black woman, you stupid, ignorant f***ing moron!" Why, Universe?

I got off the phone and cried. I am so tired of being judged, criticized, and not measuring up to some asinine, ridiculous black stereotype, while at the same time, being judged and criticized for sounding and behaving like some other asinine, ridiculous white stereotype!

I hate learning and growing sometimes, I really do. I didn't know how much hearing "you sound like a white woman" could still reduce me to tears. I had no idea this pain needed to be released. There is nothing shameful about the colour of my skin in relation to how I speak or act.

And the next time I'm asked this question? At this moment, I'm too angry to write a polite answer – great – more releasing! Smile. Seriously though, Universe, enough for a bit, ok?

July 2020

Monday

Apparently, the Universe didn't get my request regarding no more facing myself for a bit.

I had that false dream again last night about John and Jane. This time, in the dream, Jane told me that my John had asked her to marry him, saying how much he loved her. The only problem was, he and I were still dating. Watching myself follow them around trying to prove their love wasn't real was embarrassing!

Lee? I know you're tired of this work. You've done almost everything you've needed to do in order to move on. Your fears are completely false! When are you going to believe that? What you've experienced may take years to fully release and heal. Please don't give up now that you're at the end, facing the beginning.

Sunday

I finally faced myself, and it was a very scary and painful (literal and physical) experience. I finally hit rock bottom. I'd called Bev to vent. I am so tired of racism in all its forms. During our conversation, I even told her that I should close my windows, draw the drapes, turn on the fans and watch TV, read, and nap for three days. I should have listened to myself.

Tuesday

Jake called today. Actually, he'd called me last week and texted me, too. I finally called him back.

Me: I'm just trying to understand why you don't consider what you said racist.

Jake: It's not racist. You just sounded like a white woman.

Me: But what does it mean to sound like a white woman?

Jake: The way you speak, colloquially.

Me: But you say "white." What is the relevance?

Jake: There's no relevance. I was joking.

Me: No. Don't do that. I'm just really trying to understand the necessity in highlighting that I sound white.

Jake: Am I the first person who's told you that?

Me: God, no. But can you see how that phrase affects me and why I find it racist?

Jake: Let's talk about something else.

Me: No worries. I'm not upset or angry. I've just really been trying to understand why people can't see beyond colour and are always judging.

Jake: You didn't grow up where I did. You don't know what racism is really like. I grew up in the United States; I've dealt with it all my life.

Me: But don't you see how you, personally, are perpetuating the racism? What does it matter how I talk?

Jake: ……………………………

My identity crisis was brought to the forefront of my mind when George Floyd was murdered, and someone said to me, "I can't even imagine what you must be going through with all this hate towards blacks. What's been your experience with racism?" I side-stepped the question because I couldn't answer it at the time.

Why not? I'll never know what it means or feels like to be black. I'll never know what it means or feels like to be white. I'll also never know what it means or feels like to be biracial. I'm none of the above, but I do experience racism from black and white people. Ignorance, unawareness, and hate have no colour – only people do. I have to surrender my anger and fight over how I'm perceived and what it means or doesn't mean.

Thursday

Um …what the hell, Universe? (Un)believable! Of course, it's believable!

There are maybe six of us waiting at a red light. The guy in front of me makes some kind of hand gesture out of his window. I see it but don't pay attention. I'm focused on looking at the lights ahead. The guy gets out of his car and starts walking towards my car, staring right at me, making hand gestures. I think, "What the (curse) is he doing?" I look in my rearview mirror, hoping to back up and turn into a store's entrance because I'm scared the guy's going to hurt me, but a car is stopped behind me. The guy is now at my window, and he yells at me, "Don't get so close to my car!" He then turns around and gets back in his car.

My car wasn't touching his car, but I was too close. Still, he got out of his car to confront me! I was terrified. Oh, Universe! Why do I keep encountering myself? Because you're still so angry.

Friday

Two days ago, I received a letter from the police regarding my aggressive driving. I'd actually completely forgotten about that. Funny, Universe. I kept the letter thinking I should include it, but I was too embarrassed. Thinking about it now, I'm still not going to share. I don't need to imagine how scared the guy must have felt because karma showed me that terror yesterday.

The other driver on that day took a picture of my license plate and reported me. The letter was not a ticket, just a record and warning of my reckless behaviour. Had it been a ticket? A fine of $110 (I think) and a few points off my licence. I'm just really having a hard time seeing myself in others' behaviour. But it's exactly as I've behaved. How many times must I write "there are no coincidences"?

Sunday

Happy Birthday, Dad.

Thursday

I started the day crying, and it was downhill from there. Lee, this is all new for you. The crying is helping you to release. You need to sit with it and give it compassion and love. That's kind of hard when all I feel is how s**tty a person I've been.

That's because you've always known you could be really mean to people. You're just facing it for the first time, and finally understanding why. As a kid, I was always embarrassed by or ashamed of my behaviour. I don't know if I was told, "You should be ashamed of your behaviour," whenever I got caught stealing. I truly don't. But I do know that I've always *felt* embarrassed or ashamed of my behaviour.

There's a lot of guilt that's being released right now. Guilt for the innocent behaviour of a child who thought she was playing a "real fun" game with a penis.

Saturday

It's not an easy undertaking, loving yourself. There's so much forgiveness and acceptance and surrendering involved. I do forgive myself for how horribly mean I was to people.

It's the acceptance and surrendering I'm having a hard time with, but maybe that's because I'm still in this particular process. I'm not sure what I expected, but I now understand that the abuse will always be a part of me, and so will the abandonment. I honestly don't know how to accept or surrender this deep-rooted pain.

Lee, it's deep-rooted, and you've been avoiding facing it for your entire life. Cut yourself some slack. I mean, seriously. You're still trying to run away, and that which you resist, persists.

You've faced worse things. That's true. My grateful message for today: *I am grateful for my body's healing abilities and regeneration process.* I am going to add the following grateful message: *I am grateful for my mind's healing abilities and regeneration process.* I may have to get a new grateful box, as it's quite full now – I keep adding to it. Thanks, Universe.

Monday

Sigh.

Last Friday, I went for my first massage to help unlock my head to lower back. Again, I really wish I'd stayed home for those three days. I actually did better than expected. But once he hit a massive knot in my upper left shoulder (which I felt all the way down to my left toes), I couldn't relax. I tried deep breathing, but nothing worked. He'd hit a nerve that was very deep, the first of those deep roots needing to be released. I think not being able to exercise for so long brought out the pain body.

From NewWorldLibrary.com:

DISSOLVING THE PAIN BODY: An excerpt from THE POWER OF NOW by Eckhart Tolle

As long as you are unable to access the power of the Now, every emotional pain that you experience leaves behind a residue of pain that lives on in you. It merges with the pain from the past, which was already there, and becomes lodged in your mind and body.

This, of course, includes the pain you suffered as a child, caused by the unconsciousness of the world into which you were born.

This accumulated pain is a negative energy field that occupies your body and mind. If you look on it as an invisible entity in its own right, you are getting quite close to the truth. It's the emotional pain-body. It has two modes of being: dormant and active…. Anything can trigger it, particularly if it resonates with a pain pattern from your past. When it is ready to awaken from its dormant stage, even a thought or an innocent remark made by someone close to you can activate it.

Some pain-bodies are obnoxious but relatively harmless, for example like a child who won't stop whining. Others are vicious and destructive monsters, true demons. Some are physically violent; many more are emotionally violent.... Thoughts and feelings you have about your life then become deeply negative and self-destructive. Illnesses and accidents are often created in this way. Some pain-bodies drive their hosts to suicide.

When you thought you knew a person and then you are suddenly confronted with this alien, nasty creature for the first time, you are in for quite a shock.... (NewWorldLibrary.com. 2016. "DISSOLVING THE PAIN BODY: An excerpt from THE POWER OF NOW by Eckhart Tolle. Last updated August 4. https://www.newworldlibrary.com/Blog/tabid/767/articleType/ArticleView/articleId/438/DISSOLVING-THE-PAIN-BODY-An-excerpt-from-THE-POWER-OF-NOW-by-Eckhart-Tolle.aspx#.YCF80-hKhPY.)

Dearest Colleen (body) and Lee (mind),

I know neither of you can see nor feel how it's possible to reconnect with each other. I promise you, though, once the two of you spend some time together and feel that you're both safe, your world changes. Together, you learn to love each other, finally becoming one. I see where you currently sit. I can't tell you how you were able to rise up, one last time and remember who you truly are. I can only tell you that you did.

Love,
Col(lee)n
(body, mind, and spirit)

Wednesday

I'm beginning to understand what created this Lee, which is part of the forgiveness, acceptance, and surrender process.

From RealLove.com:

What is real love?

The REAL question is, "What is Unconditional Love?" That is so different from what most people have ever known that we're going to call it Real Love. Real Love is unconditional love. THAT is the kind of "love" we all want. In Real Love there is no disappointment, impatience, irritation, or anger. Wow, now that is different—so different that most people have never truly felt it. (RealLove.com. 2020. "What is real love?" https://reallove.com/what-is-real-love/.)

It's not easy learning to love yourself unconditionally, let alone another.

Friday

I was talking to someone today, and when I told them how much better I felt from all the learning, wisdom, and understanding I'd recently gone through, he didn't believe me. I get it. He's had many, many negative experiences with me. He said, "One day, you're fine, the next day you're angry or sad. I never know who to expect when we meet. There's no way you could just overcome that. Today, you're just having a good day. Tomorrow?" Tomorrow, I'll be learning how to respond from my beingness.

CHAPTER 2

Learning How to Love, Believe, and Have Faith and Trust in Myself

September 2020

Saturday

And now, we enter the best month of them *all*, my month! I truly love my birthday. I always have.

Monday

I think I passed a test today, and I'm very proud of myself. It has to do with apartment laundry etiquette. I remember the first time someone took my clothes out of the washer when I went down ten minutes late. I learned that lesson well. Yes, it is gross when other people touch your clothes, but there's no law against it, nor does it involve either of our rights. I was calm and apologetic in the face of anger and outrage. As for apartment laundry etiquette? Thirty minutes to wash and one hour to dry. Watch your clock.

Saturday

From Happify.com:

6 Ways to Forgive Yourself and Start Moving Forward

There's often no way to undo past mistakes, but you can make amends with them. The below process for responsible self-forgiveness, which Everett L. Worthington Jr., Ph.D., details in his book, Moving Forward: Six Steps to Forgiving Yourself and Breaking Free from the Past, will help you learn to be kind to yourself, one step at a time.

Step 1: Receive Forgiveness from the Universe

Take a step back and look at the big picture, not just those guilt-inspiring moments of your life. Remind yourself that everyone makes mistakes, and that you, too, deserve to be forgiven. If you have a spiritual practice, revisiting your teachings and growing your connection with your beliefs can also help you let go.

Step 5: Embrace Self-Acceptance

Even after you've forgiven yourself, you may have a hard time coming to terms with your past mistakes. Accept what you can't change. Remind yourself that actions don't define who you are. Getting stuck in the past makes it impossible to move forward to a better future. (Jessica Cassity. Happify.com. 2020. "6 Ways to Forgive Yourself and Start Moving Forward." https://www.happify.com/hd/6-ways-to-forgive-yourself/)

Monday

There's this dress I bought five years ago that I absolutely love! It makes me happy just looking at it! Unfortunately, I never fit into the dress again after buying it. Why? I'd bought it after my return from the Caribbean when I'd lost so much weight. I put it on yesterday, and it almost zips up. Almost. Anytime I do a meditation that asks you to picture being your future self, this is what I picture: I'm living somewhere really warm in a beautiful duplex with an ocean view. In the morning, I go to yoga, do some work on the computer, and am now getting ready to go for lunch with my friends at our spot. I put on this dress, do a twirl, and laugh. I get my dog leashed up (saying goodbye to Kya and Bowie) and head out the door for a thirty-minute scenic view along the boardwalk. I feel overjoyed with love and appreciation! I'm going to wear this dress on my upcoming birthday. I started doing yoga again, and it feels wonderful!

Wednesday

I just watched the Oprah interview with Lady Gaga from January 2020. I was shocked by her story. I knew she'd been bullied in high school, but didn't know she'd been repeatedly raped at nineteen. In my opinion, she's an incredibly brave, multi-talented, inspirational, and beautiful being.

Lady Gaga talked about her tormenting bullies once picking her up and dumping her in a trash bin. She said she'd never received therapy or help for the rape trauma (repeatedly raped), which she says caused her post-traumatic stress disorder. After years of suppressing her physical and emotional pain, Lady Gaga had a psychotic break. How did she begin to heal? Lady Gaga said "Radical acceptance was key. Also being open to medication and also being open to talking about my trauma. It's one of the hardest things that any human can face. And it's a lot easier to go home and have a bottle of wine or two or three, right? Just numb it all away, or dig deep."

Lady Gaga also said "I do believe that this happened for a reason. All the things I've been through, I think, they were supposed to happen. I was supposed to go through this – even the rape, all of it. I think I was supposed to go through all of these things. I radically accepted they happened. And I think it happened because God was saying to me, 'I'm going to show you pain, and then you're going to help other people who are in pain because you understand it.'"

Is Lady Gaga now living in pure bliss? Very realistically, Lady Gaga said, "Well, you know, some days are better than others. Some days I have lots of self-love. Some days I have less. Some days I have lots of self-confidence, some days I have less. But I had to radically just accept that. Every day can be different, and that's ok. It doesn't mean we're not moving forward."

Thursday

I've been contemplating all that Lady Gaga said. A key element to Lady Gaga's healing was the team of doctors she had at her disposal. And that's the crux of the mental health crisis: a team is needed, and there's "no funding available." Really?

From The Planetary Society:

NASA's FY 2020 Budget

NASA's budget in fiscal year (FY) 2020 is $22.629 billion which represents 0.48% of all U.S. government spending. This is a 5.3% increase from the previous fiscal year.

The White House released its Presidential Budget Request (PBR) for NASA's fiscal year 2020 on 11 March 2019, followed by a supplemental budget request on 13 May. Together they proposed a top-line NASA budget of $22.6 billion—a 5% increase compared to the previous year. The supplemental request was released in response to a Presidential directive to land astronauts on the Moon by 2024. (The Planetary Society. 2020. "NASA's FY 2020 Budget." https://www.planetary.org/space-policy/ nasas-fy-2020-budget)

In my opinion, spending $22.6 *billion* to destroy, pollute, and interfere with the Universe is a crime.

According to Rubina Kapil in her Mental Health First Aid February 6, 2019 online article, in the United States, "almost half of adults (46.4 percent) will experience a mental illness during their lifetime. 5 percent of adults (18 or older) experience a mental illness in any one year, equivalent to 43.8 million people."

Caren Howard, MHA Advocacy Manager, in a Mental Health America online article, "How Trump's Budget Will Affect People With Mental Health Conditions" says, "The Fiscal Year 2019 budget requests $68.4 billion for the Department of Health and Human Services (HHS), which is a $17.9 billion (or 21 percent) decrease from the 2017 enacted level."

I think NASA's budget could help with the mental health crisis. I appreciate that we're explorers and want to know what's beyond. But what's beyond the underlying causes of mental health disorders needs to be explored.

Lady Gaga used the terminology "radical acceptance" or "radically accepted" quite frequently. I get why. The Cambridge Dictionary online defines radical as "believing or expressing the belief that there should be great or extreme social or political change." I'd like to amend that definition to: Radical: believing or expressing the belief that there must be great and extreme personal change first, and then social and political change will occur.

When Lady Gaga said she could be triggered any time, by any thing, I knew exactly what she meant. And as Karma would have it, I was triggered today. I went to a store I always go to. The owner is a sweet older man, always with a smile (albeit now masked) and warm greeting – someone who puts a smile on your face. As I tapped my card on the machine, he placed his hand on top of mine and said, "Have a great day!" I flinched at his touch and froze inside. I removed my hand quickly, smiled, and said, "Have a great day, as well!" as my mind repeated, "Why did he touch me? I don't like being touched! He shouldn't have touched me!" all the way out the door and into my car. I actually do like being touched, and on another day, it might not have bothered me.

I was unaware of my misunderstanding and unrealistic expectations of how life would be once I'd dealt with my past. When I "radically" accepted that the abuse and abandonment would always be a part of me, that understanding was profound. Lady Gaga said, "We are going to solve this mental health crisis." There is most definitely a mental health crisis in the world.

However, there is also a mental health crisis directly caused by the sexual abuse crisis in the world. I just think sexual abuse needs its own, specialized illness category. Yes, but Lee, wouldn't you then need a separate category for physical, verbal, etc., abuse? Exactly.

We all have different brains that process trauma differently. Lady Gaga assembled a team of the best doctors because she could afford to. It always comes down to money. A piece of paper is worth more than an individual's life. Lady Gaga reiterated emphatically that her method and medications would not work on anyone else. (Lady Gaga says that the amount of medications she takes when put all together sounds like a baby rattle.) Each individual requires their own personal team. That's the reality of having a mental sexual health issue. One size will never fit all.

I wonder how many individuals' lives would or could be saved if an additional 22.6 billion was allotted to the mental health industry, especially now, with the newly created Covid-19 mental illness.

From GlobalNews.ca:

Mental health effects of the coronavirus pandemic will be 'severe,' expert warns

Federal and provincial governments need to prepare for a swell in mental health problems caused by the coronavirus pandemic, which one expert warns will pose a "severe" challenge in managing.

"There's a real recognition that the mental health impacts are going to be severe," said Margaret Eaton.

Eaton pointed to Nova Scotia as an example of one of the places where her organization is seeing a spike in the number of people asking for mental health help.

She said while branches in that province would normally see around 25 phone calls per day, they recently received 700 in a single 24-hour period. (Amanda Connolly. Global News. 2020. "Mental health effects of the coronavirus pandemic will be 'severe,' expert warns." Last updated May 10. https://globalnews.ca/news/6922614/coronavirus-mental-health-impacts/.)

Friday

People can be so sweet!

I always smile and chat with the people at the drive-thru where I get my coffee. There's this one guy in particular whose energy is so upbeat and positive, you can't help but feel good after being, briefly, in his company. When he gave me my coffee this morning, he asked me if I liked chocolate and presented me with a sweet surprise: a chocolate chip heart cookie! Such a small gesture put the biggest smile on my face and in my heart that I'm still feeling! Thanks, Universe!

I am in the process of believing and radically accepting that everything needed to happen exactly as it did in my life, so I could remember who I truly am. Lady Gaga also emphasized gratitude's power. Today's grateful message: *I am grateful for my car.* Whether it's a chocolate chip heart cookie or a car, I am grateful.

Tuesday

I did not have the happiest birthday and never came close to feeling overjoyed with love and appreciation. I did, however, see my sister. We spoke for one minute, after years of no contact, about something specific, and then I turned and walked away. On the drive home, I cried. When I got home, I cried. Lots and lots of emotions.

Wednesday

I'm not ready to talk about yesterday's encounter.

Friday

Like Lady Gaga, I too believe that everything happens for a reason. Ten minutes after I was born, the Universe whispered to me: My dearest child, from this moment onward, you'll be faced with an incredible amount of pain and loss. There will be nobody who understands you or protects you. You'll believe you're all alone in this world and contemplate whether life is worth living. But you made a promise to me, my dearest child, before you were born. You promised me you'd remember that I would never leave your side; that you are love; that you are a creative being; and that together, we can create miracles.

Sunday

Today's grateful message: *I am grateful for the wisdom my experiences have taught me.* Thank you, Universe.

Wednesday

I'm still feeling emotional after seeing my sister. Such is the reality of being human.

October 2020

Thursday

I was told to watch Netflix's *The Social Dilemma*. I would highly suggest that everyone watch this documentary. It's very scary indeed. TV advertising drove me to Netflix. I absolutely loathe commercials. It's a billion-dollar-mind-manipulating industry. And it lies to you, constantly and effectively.

Excerpt from *The Social Dilemma*. Speaking is Tristan Harris, Google Former Design Ethicist, Co-Founder of Centre for Humane Technology: "If we don't agree on what is true, or that there is such a thing as truth, we're toast. This is the problem, beneath other problems. Because if we can't agree on what's true, then we can't navigate out of any of our problems."

What's true is that we've all forgotten how to love ourselves. This is the problem beneath all of our problems. This is at the heart of humanity.

Wednesday

Time to come clean.

I caused a car accident. (No one was hurt, thankfully.) Sigh. On Tuesday, I was driving home from seeing my first movie post-Covid19. I'd had the entire theatre to myself! My thoughts turned to my sister, and I was lost, driving on autopilot. What really happened between us? Where did I go wrong, for her? Why couldn't she even have wished me a happy birthday in that one minute (even though I didn't give her a chance because I turned and walked away after the miscommunication was cleared up). It really hadn't been necessary to see her, yet I insisted. Why did I put myself through that? Why? Why? Why? And on and on.

I was approaching the turn to my building's parking lot, literally six seconds from my parking spot. There was a truck just passing the parking lot entrance, so I slowed a bit, and when the truck moved forward again, I turned, but the truck stopped again, just as I turned, and I heard "crunch." What the hell? I was sure I had just nicked him, but I stopped (a mere four seconds from my parking spot). I went to check my side mirror to see if any traffic was coming, but my side mirror was broken and dangling. Huh? I went to open my door but it wouldn't open all the way. Are you kidding me?

I exchanged insurance information with the man and drove into my parking spot. I called the insurance company and got that sorted. The next day, I brought my car to the insurance company's collision centre and asked the agent to guesstimate the damage to my car – around $2000, he thought. I picked up my rental there too. I was obviously so angry with myself for having been so absentminded, and grateful that no one got hurt because of my absentmindedness.

I knew it was a lesson, so I accepted it and calmed down.

Last Monday, the insurance company sent me an email saying the car had been deemed a loss. I'm sorry, what now? No, that can't be true. I was still able to drive the car. The actual cost of the damage was under $4000 and so wasn't worth fixing (even though there was no structural damage, but once they opened the hood, who knew?). I'd be given a cheque for under $5000. I cried but accepted it and went out to look for a new used car. Unfortunately, there was nothing under $8000 – unless I wanted to buy my car on some side-street used car lot. I did that with this car and was taken, badly. I really was sold a lemon, but I paid lots and lots for it not to be a lemon.

After speaking with someone, I decided to ask the garage that saved my car from its lemon state if the damage could be fixed. They told me they believed so and took the car into the garage, hoisted it up, looked under the hood, and found no damage. It was all cosmetic. They said it would cost under $1000 to fix. Why such a difference in price between replace and fix?

The collision center wanted to replace everything – something about a standard of safety to adhere to. My garage was able to find a similar red panel for my door and will work out any dents, still all the while maintaining a standard of safety.

I told my insurance company I'd have my car fixed on my own and received a cheque from the insurance company for over $3000. How can any of that make sense? No, my car's not worth much, but I own it outright. Why wouldn't the insurance company just pay the $1000 or so to fix my car?

All this drama I created for myself (and others) because I didn't deal with my complicated emotions after seeing my sister after years of silence. (The accident happened three weeks to the day of seeing her.) And my lower back? Ouch! I wasn't hurt in the accident at all, but the stress of keeping all those feelings and emotions buried refused to be ignored.

Thursday

On Tuesday, I got together with my friends for our monthly gabfest. I shared how my emotions were still all over the place (I had to wave the tears off) after encountering my sister. They were incredibly supportive. One said, "Oh no, you feel as if you're back to square one again." I've been thinking about that and I'm not back to square one at all. Rather, I'm on the last square.

Today, my horoscope talked about letting go of an old grievance. I'd never even considered that my relationship with my sister could be thought of as an old grievance. Yes, I am ready to surrender this "old grievance." Thanks, Universe.

Friday

A radio host was commenting on Chris Hadfield's recent video on his talk of soon being able to live on the Moon. Chris Hadfield is a retired Canadian astronaut, engineer, and former Royal Canadian Air Force fighter pilot. The first Canadian to walk in space, Hadfield has flown two Space Shuttle missions and served as commander of the International Space Station (ISS).

I listened to the host summarize what Mr. Hadfield said and decided I should watch his video for myself. I found it on YouTube.

I'd read before that the cost of going to space had dramatically decreased, but it still costs hundreds of millions of dollars. Mr. Hadfield said that on the Moon, the sun never stops shining, and there are unlimited reserves of water. He also said, "And that's where we are in history. It's pretty interesting. Instead of just living on Earth, we also live on the Moon. Living on the Moon is going to be an international endeavour.

There's already Chinese hardware on the Moon, the United States is going with NASA, Israel had been working to land on the Moon, India is working to land on the Moon. A lot of leading nations of the world, including Canada...."

I wish people wouldn't think this way. We have everything we need right here, on planet Earth. We're destroying Earth, so the solution is to live on the Moon too? How exactly would that look, with the same warring nations on Earth also inhabiting the Moon? International endeavours? That's worked out so well for planet Earth. It's the people, not the place. And, wherever you go, there you are.

If you want to save Earth, you've got to think outside the box, but not to outer space. In my hometown today, it was announced we're back in a semi-lockdown because Covid-19 cases are wildly rising. Forget international endeavours, how about human co-operation? Why are there pandemics, viruses, and diseases? Because of humans. I can only imagine what manmade pandemics, viruses, and diseases will be created on the Moon.

Statistics have shown how the Earth was able to start to heal and repair when we were in full lockdown:

From HindustanTimes.com:

Earth Day: How the planet healed during Covid-19 lockdown

CRISIS The entire country is under lockdown since last one month, and nature has found a way to let Earth regain its lost wealth, during this period.

The news of pink flamingoes return in huge numbers to Mumbai beach is certainly something to rejoice about. The reduction in intensity of human activities at and around the city is being touted as a major reason for the possibility of flamingos to flock the city in such large numbers. The Bombay Natural History Society has stated that their number is 25% more than it was in the last year. (Ruchika Garg. Hindustan Times. 2020. "Earth Day: How the planet healed during Covid-19 lockdown." Last modified April 22. https://www.hindustantimes.com/coronavirus-crisis/earth-day-how-the-planet-healed-during-covid-19-lockdown/story-Rp7JnPzowHlfj6kIkH03BI.html.)

From GQmiddleeast.com:

Is The Coronavirus Lockdown Actually Healing The Planet?

In China, where the first cases of coronavirus were detected, a massive decline in pollution and greenhouse gases have now been recorded. Satellite images on NASA's website show how the decrease in industrial, business and transportation activity between January and February 2020 has reduced the levels of atmospheric nitrogen dioxide (No2) first in Wuhan and then across the country. "This is the first time I have seen such a dramatic drop-off over such a wide area for a specific event," Fei Liu, an air quality researcher at NASA's Goddard Space Flight Centre, said in a statement.

These improvements in nature, albeit due to human restriction, are inevitably something to take note of. If there is one thing this pandemic has proven it is that human activity is the foremost cause of pollution on earth. This is proof that if we want, the human race can work together towards a sustainable future.

(Yaseen Dockrat. GQmiddleeast.com. 2020. "Is The Coronavirus Lockdown Actually Healing The Planet?" Last modified March 2020. https://www.gqmiddleeast.com/culture/is-the-coronavirus-lockdown-actually-healing-the-planet.)

I think what bothered me most about Mr. Hadfield's comments were "has unlimited power supply and basically a deep, deep reserve of water, then all that really remains for us is to build…and we can start living there."

He could be describing planet Earth, once upon a time. Whether it's racism, women's rights, immigration, or planet Earth, we keep revolving and not evolving. For the first time in history, we have an opportunity to radically change our way of living and heal ourselves and our planet. It's an individual and collective endeavour that would evolve the world.

Saturday

Do you know what today is?

I didn't until my radio station told me. It's World Mental Health Day. How apropos. Why?

My mental health has, finally, stabilized. I still have more releasing to do. I know and accept this. I've been sage-cleansing myself every day for the past week and will continue to for however long I need to.

Sunday

As there are no coincidences, today's grateful message: *I am grateful for the time I've been given to learn and love myself.* Thanks, Universe.

Friday

I saw this on my newsfeed today from Space.com:

Phew! 2 big hunks of space junk zoom safely past each other in near-miss

The chance of a collision was higher than 10%, according to LeoLabs.

It looks like humanity just dodged a pretty big space-junk bullet.

Two large pieces of orbital debris — a defunct Soviet navigation satellite and a spent Chinese rocket body — apparently whizzed safely past each other high over the South Atlantic Ocean on Thursday evening (Oct. 15).

Orbital collisions are not just the stuff of science-fiction films like 2013's "Gravity." In 2009, for instance, a defunct Russian military satellite called Kosmos 2251 slammed into the operational communications satellite Iridium 33, generating 1,800 pieces of trackable debris by the following October (and many others too small to monitor).

The debris problem will continue to grow as more and more satellites launch to space — a trend that's accelerating, thanks to continuing decreases in the costs of both launch and satellite development. And the problem could get out of hand, seriously threatening spaceflight and exploration activities, if we don't start tackling it now, many experts say. (Mike Wall. Space.com. 2020. "Phew! 2 big hunks of space junk zoom safely past each other in near-miss." Last modified October 2020. https://www.space.com/dead-chinese-russian-space-junk-near-miss-leolabs.)

From PopularMechanics.com:

Two Dead Satellites Could've Collided Last Night. Thankfully, They Didn't. That would've been very, very bad.

This exact scenario is one that spaceflight experts have been warning about for decades. Earth is shrouded in a web of space junk, with pieces ranging in size from flecks of paint to spent rocket stages. The United States Space Surveillance Network is currently monitoring roughly 200,000 objects between 0.4 and 4 inches, 14,000 objects larger than 4 inches, and thousands of larger objects. (Jennifer Leman. PopularMechanics.com. 2020. "Two Dead Satellites Could've Collided Last Night. Thankfully, They Didn't. That would've been very, very bad." Last modified October 15. https://www.popularmechanics.com/space/satellites/a34383707/space-junk-collision-risks/.)

In my opinion, we should all be outraged by the concept of space junk. Why am I harping on this so much? Because it's going to take hundreds of millions (billions?) of dollars to clear and clean out the space debris that humans created, and still, space will never be clear or clean again, just like our oceans and planet currently stand – full of our debris.

All that money and technology could be used for mental health discoveries. There is a way to decrease this mental health crisis, but it requires billions of dollars to do so: rebuild psychiatric hospitals and acknowledge that an individual recovering from recent or current trauma requires several different types of therapy. Perhaps this would help some of the debris of humans living on the streets around the world.

I think only psychologists or psychiatrists should be allowed to prescribe medication along with regular therapy sessions, be they weekly, bi-weekly, or monthly. That would include yourself, Lee. Yes, I know. Someone told me that they too had to walk away from their family (helped me to know I had to do the same) but that it took them over a dozen years to be truly healed from this traumatic experience. I'm on year five, and I radically accept it may take me many more years. It would be wonderful to talk to a professional about this and other things I've not shared here. I will eventually work them all out, but how much quicker would these releases and healing be if I could talk with someone weekly? Unfortunately, I don't have that type of insurance coverage. I have no issue being on medication, but eventually, the goal is to not need it. Shouldn't that be everyone's goal? Some people will always need to be on medication, and there's nothing wrong with that. Recently, a friend told me they were put on medication by their family doctor after experiencing panic attacks for the first time in their life. When I asked if their family doctor had suggested therapy, they told me that hadn't even been mentioned to them. They were to return to their family doctor in a month (or sooner if they experienced adverse side-effects) for more medication. It's awesome that they're feeling better now that they're on medication, but what about healing the cause of the anxiety?

It's a mental health crisis for a reason. If our mind and body are no longer in sync, we're at war within ourselves. How are your body and mind?

(HAPTER 3

Knowing I Love Myself, I Am Perfect, I Am Whole, and I Am Complete

November 2020

Saturday

At the beginning of this journey, I said my self-help book would be different. Has it been?

Yes, absolutely. Why? Because it's been *my* self-help book. I've shared with you all that I had to go through in order to learn how to love myself. I can't even believe some of my experiences!

I know we all want to be told how to learn to love ourselves, but unless you're me, with my specific history and beliefs, how can I tell you what to do? Do you believe in your horoscopes? Do you believe in sage cleansing (which I've been doing every night for the past week)? Do you believe in energy stones? (I can feel the weight of my strength and love stones currently in my pocket.) Do you believe in inspirational tattoos? (I've got Faith, To Do One's Best, and Thanks Universe, among others.) Do you believe you're here for a reason? Do you believe in the Universe guiding you? Do you believe in a grateful box? Do you believe the Universe sends you signs?

Today's grateful message: *I am grateful for all the signs the Universe is sending me.*

I can't tell you whether or not you need to walk away from your family. Your family may love and support you. There is only one thing I can tell you to do in order to love yourself: Know thyself. And I do mean, *all* of thyself.

The cover of my book screams at you, which is what we're used to. Inside, the right side forces you to look closer, which we're not used to regarding ourselves.

It's one of the scariest and most painful experiences to unlock and unravel who you've become and why. But unless and until you do that, how can you radically accept that you are the love you seek? You are worthy. You are good enough. You do matter.

For months, I've been trying to get to this last chapter. I tried three different times to write it, but it didn't feel right. I couldn't start this final chapter until I knew it to be true. The one-minute encounter on my birthday was my catalyst. How can I tell you what your catalyst needs to be?

The only thing I *can* tell you to do is this: Question everything about yourself. Underneath your trauma, you're someone else. That's what you need to remember.

There is no preparation for what will be experienced on your own journey to self-love. Just be prepared to radically accept every experience that's required of you to discover the eternal love you have for yourself.

Sunday

I'd love to be able to say I'm now living a life of pure bliss. Isn't that what we expect from self-help books? What I can tell you is the truth. My mind is no longer consumed with old grievances. I know it sounds so basic, yet it's anything but. If you'd asked me four months ago how I thought I'd feel about my family eight months from now, the answer would have been: hurt and betrayed. That's because I couldn't see past my pain, or more accurately, I didn't know how to see past the pain.

Last week, I burnt my knuckle badly on the oven rack. Man, it hurt like crazy! I wore a bandage for several days and watched it bubble and blister. When I finally went bandage-free on Thursday, it was still raw, red, and hurt. (Someone even asked me what happened to my knuckle, as it looked very pain-ful.) On Friday, the pain was gone, but I wondered how long it would take to heal, and if I should put the bandage back on for appearance's sake. Yesterday, the burn area had turned from red to pink, and the burnt skin was peeling off. Today, I can see a major improvement on how the scar now looks. We can see so clearly the body's healing abilities.

The mind's healing abilities aren't so clearly seen. They are felt from within. And they require more time to heal because the mind tricks you into believing no progress is being made. When I felt that my mind wasn't frantically trying to run any-more (literally and figuratively – my family and I live in the same city), I felt lighter inside. Being molested will never be an old grievance, but my experience of how my family has reacted, is. I am no longer living from fear – that's what I meant regard-ing my mental health stabilizing.

Monday

It's going to be very strange tomorrow, not writing.

I'd had this idea of how long this chapter needed to be, but there's nothing more to write – not here, at least. I know I am perfect, whole, and complete all on my own, and I love myself for knowing and feeling this truth.

The remembering has already begun, and with that comes the magnificent, magical, and incredible power within me to cocreate my dreams. I love you, Universe.

With every donation, a voice will be given to
the creativity that lies within the hearts of
our children living with diverse challenges.

By making this difference, children that may
not have been given the opportunity to have their
Heart Heard will have the freedom to create
beautiful works of art and musical creations.

Donate by visiting

HeartstobeHeard.com

We thank you.